Moneylenders and Their Customers

Karen Rowlingson

POLICY STUDIES INSTITUTE
London

PUBLISHING

The publishing imprint of the independent
POLICY STUDIES INSTITUTE
100 Park Village East, London NW1 3SR
Telephone: 071-387 2171 Fax: 071-388 0914

ISBN 0 85374 654 0

PSI Research Report 793

A CIP catalogue record of this book is available from the British Library.

1 2 3 4 5 6 7 8 9

PSI publications are available from
BEBC Distribution Ltd
P O Box 1496, Poole, Dorset, BH12 3YD

Books will normally be despatched within 24 hours. Cheques should be made payable
to BEBC Distribution Ltd.

Credit card and telephone/fax orders may be placed on the following freephone
numbers:

FREEPHONE: 0800 262260
FREEFAX: 0800 262266

Booktrade representation (UK & Eire):
Broadcast Books
24 De Montfort Road, London SW16 1LW
Telephone: 081-677 5129

PSI subscriptions are available from PSI's subscription agent
Carfax Publishing Company Ltd
P O Box 25, Abingdon, Oxford OX14 3UE

Laserset by Policy Studies Institute
Printed in Great Britain by Latimer Trend, Plymouth

Acknowledgements

First and foremost, I would like to thank Elaine Kempson at PSI for all her help during the study.

The Joseph Rowntree Foundation provided the resources for this project and also granted some additional funds for disseminating the results. Derek Williams at the Foundation has been a constant source of encouragement throughout the research.

The study's advisory group provided very practical guidance which greatly improved the study. The members of the advisory group were Janet Ford, Deborah Khudabux, Dan Murphy, Jan Pahl and Jane Ritchie.

The research could not have taken place without the cooperation of CCA UK and all the companies, collectors and customers who took part in the study. The need to preserve confidentiality prevents me from naming them here but my gratitude goes out to them all.

The fieldwork for this study meant that I was away from home for many weeks – often at very inconvenient times. I would like to thank my husband, Stephen McKay, for holding the fort and providing moral support during this and all my other research projects.

Contents

Introduction

The image of a moneylender is often one of a 'loanshark', lending money at extortionate rates of interest and preying on the poorest sections of the community with the use of threats and actual violence. The media reinforces this image by focusing on the worst cases of illegal moneylending (for example, a Channel 4 'Cutting Edge' programme on 'Loansharks' shown in 1993).

The image is a powerful one. But the trade association for licensed moneylenders, the Consumer Credit Association of the United Kingdom (CCA), denies its accuracy for licensed, legal money-lending. Until now, there have been no independent studies in the UK which have assessed the role and nature of moneylending. With this in mind, the Policy Studies Institute has carried out a study, funded by the Joseph Rowntree Foundation.

The aim of the research was to provide an independent assessment of *licensed* moneylending in the UK, by observing moneylenders in the course of their business and then interviewing them and their customers independently. Such an assessment is needed because of the many criticisms of moneylending and the lack of research evidence.

A detailed, qualitative study was necessary in order to investigate the nature of the relationship between moneylenders and their customers. This involved observation work with eight moneylenders from six companies. During this observation work, data from about 500 interactions with customers was collected. Detailed interviews with managers, moneylenders and 31 customers also took place.

Summary of Findings

Cultural views of moneylending are extremely negative. Religious disapproval of charging any interest on loans has now been replaced by condemnation of 'extortionate' interest. Some forms of credit are thought to be 'socially harmful' due to the amount of repayments and the use of 'deceit or oppression' in contracting the agreement. But there is no precise definition of what is meant by 'socially harmful' or what constitutes 'extortionate' interest.

Moneylending companies

There are currently about 1200 licensed moneylending companies in Britain, 800 of which are members of the Consumer Credit Association of the United Kingdom. The companies range dramatically in size from the six giants, the largest of which employs over 8,000 agents to the 400 or so very small companies with only one or two collectors. Most companies deal mainly in cash loans but some also sell goods and vouchers on credit. APRs vary most according to the length of loan. With loans of the same length, there is some difference between companies' rates of charge. With APRs varying from 100 to 500 per cent, credit from a moneylender is far more expensive than credit from mainstream lenders.

Moneylending collectors

There are about 27,000 people who lend and collect from door-to-door each week. These divide into two types. The majority work as self-employed agents for moneylending companies. Most of these are women. The remaining collectors run their own companies and sometimes employ one or two other collectors apart from themselves.

Companies and managers in the study tried to recruit agents who could get on well with customers but who could also detach themselves sufficiently and maintain loyalty to the interests of the company. Being sociable and friendly was very important. Agents who were not liked or trusted by customers would probably not be successful since, it was implied, customers could go to another company or simply stop using their company.

People became agents because they were attracted to the the hours of work, the pay, the opportunities of self-employment and the interaction with people. They were usually recruited through personal recommendation or advertising. In terms of their social class, age and sex, they reflected the philosophies of the companies employing them. Some were very similar to their customers. Others were from slightly more middle class backgrounds. This sometimes caused friction between themselves and their customers.

Agents generally worked on a self-employed basis, being paid commission on the amount they collected.

People became owners of small moneylending businesses because they were entrepreneurs who were interested in the credit industry or in sales. The owner-collectors were the least like their customers in terms of social class but this difference did not cause much friction as there was some acceptance and respect between them and their customers.

The typical week for all collectors ran from Thursday to Tuesday including some evenings and Saturday work. The amount of time spent with customers depended on a combination of two factors: how much the collector liked the customer and how much they were 'worth' in commercial terms.

Images of moneylenders often show them to be exploiting vulnerable people. But in many ways, they themselves are vulnerable. Three out of the eight collectors in the study had personally been attacked by strangers for their money. Two had been attacked by customers' dogs.

Moneylending customers
There are about 3 million customers of moneylending companies in the UK.

The 31 customers interviewed had started using moneylenders at different stages of their lifecycle. Most were couples with young children when they first borrowed from a moneylender. The male partner in the couple was usually in low-paid manual employment. Some new customers were young, single people, in work but still living at home with their families. A few came from other groups such as lone parents, older single people or older couples with no dependants.

Moneylenders were reluctant to take on very poor people as customers. Those groups with a restricted access to licensed moneylending included the long-term unemployed, lone parents, pensioners and those living in areas with a crime problem.

Although new customers' financial situations were relatively sound, these situations often changed over time. Of the 31 customers interviewed, nine were now in couples with dependent children, five were in couples of working age without dependants, four were lone parents, three were older, single, disabled people and ten were over pension age. Most of the couples who were of working age had at least one full-time paid worker in the family. But most of this work was relatively low-paid, manual work. Most of the lone parents and pensioners were living above income support levels through sources such as maintenance from ex-partners, income from work, occupational pensions and disability benefits. But they were, nevertheless, still living on very low incomes. Although the sample was chosen to generally reflect the demographic mix of all customers, it is not completely representative. For example, the proportion of pensioners interviewed is probably greater than the actual proportion of customers who are pensioners.

Some customers, such as couples without dependants, used credit from a moneylender to purchase consumer goods. But those whose situations had deteriorated began to borrow from a moneylender to pay for essentials such as the gas or electricity bill.

Reasons why people use moneylenders

Credit from a moneylender is very expensive and much more expensive than other types of credit. So why do 3 million people use it?

Most new customers identified a need, such as clothing, and then decided to use a moneylender to satisfy that need. Most of these people would probably have found it difficult to get credit from most other sources. Although many were in work, that work was often casual and low-paid. Most were council tenants and so their housing tenure would be a negative indicator on any application credit scoring, the technique used by most creditors such as banks and finance houses.

But, in any case, few of these people actually applied for other sources of credit. This was for various reasons. Some hardly considered the options. They decided to borrow from the moneylender because they had been used and recommended by parents or friends. Some did consider other sources but felt that they were unsuitable because they preferred to use cash and did not want a large loan which would incur large monthly repayments. Some considered other sources to be suitable but thought that they would be turned down and so did not attempt an application. One person did apply for a bank loan and was rejected, turning instead to moneylending. Most of these people were not desperate for money but preferred to use credit rather than wait or try, with difficulty, to save. A few were turning to a moneylender because they felt they had little alternative and were in great need.

Other new customers were encouraged to identify needs by canvassers who called at their door, selling various goods. These people were informed that they could pay for the item they 'needed' by instalments and so they became a customer of a moneylender. Those who bought from canvassers only had one option – to buy from the canvasser or not.

Other new customers were aware that they could get a loan from a moneylender because their family used this source of credit. They decided to borrow some money and only then decided exactly what to do with it. These people did not really consider other sources of credit. Their families had used a moneylender in the past without any serious problems and so it seemed a sensible way of financing expenditure on clothes and other consumer durables. They probably would have had some difficulty gaining credit from other sources, but few considered it.

Customers knew that credit from a moneylender was more expensive than other forms of credit but they did not necessarily understand *how much* more expensive it was. This was because they did not use the APR in considering the cost of credit. They looked at the amount of money they were being charged as a proportion of the principal amount. For example, if they borrowed £100 and were charged £30, they would say that the interest rate was 30 per cent. Such a calculation does not take into account the time period over which the money was borrowed – an essential factor in assessing the relative cost of credit. If such a loan was repaid over a fairly typical period, such as 20 weeks, the APR would actually be over 300 per cent.

Although customers had few alternatives and knew that they were paying dearly for credit, they also saw many advantages to borrowing from a moneylender. For example, they could borrow relatively small sums of money and have repayments collected from them on a weekly basis at a convenient time. In a sense, borrowing from a moneylender was seen as an alternative to saving because while it was always difficult to put money away each week, the knowledge that a collector would be knocking at the door was an extra incentive to ensure that the money was there. But if they did miss the odd payment, there were no default charges.

The borrowing and lending process

Some people had got into a habit of borrowing from a moneylender and automatically took out a loan when they came to the end of their current loan. For some, this was because they were happy using the service of a moneylender. For others, it was because they were in great need of the money.

Moneylenders used various subtle techniques to encourage borrowing. Some took brochures, catalogues and samples of goods around to the customer as they came close to the end of a loan. Some tried to identify needs that the customer might have through observing their home situation and talking to them. Generally, moneylenders used a combination of charm and cheek to encourage further borrowing. But they were treading a fine line. Customers generally stopped using pushy moneylenders. Some collectors also used manipulation to encourage custom. They made it well known that their commission depended on sales and that they needed to reach certain sales targets. Customers generally liked their collectors and so wanted to help them out by borrowing.

It was the better-off customers and those who paid regularly who were most likely to be encouraged to borrow. Other customers were sometimes discouraged if they were having difficulty repaying what they already owed. But collectors were subject to pressures from managers to increase sales and there was a fear that if someone was refused a loan then they would go elsewhere.

Most customers had some difficulties repaying their loans. About a third sometimes missed payments and another third were either paying reduced amounts or were regularly paying but had difficulty finding the money. Those who had most difficulty included pensioners who were borrowing to pay for bills and essentials and were paying out a large proportion of their income on repayments. Older working couples who were borrowing for consumer goods and only paying a small proportion of their income in loan repayments had fewest difficulties.

Collectors accepted that their customers would miss payments from time to time. They rarely said anything to a customer who said they could not pay that week. And if someone took longer to pay than the originally agreed time, no extra charge or interest was added. If someone did miss payments, the company would send a letter and sometimes the manager would visit to see why this was happening and what could be done. Companies saw little merit in going to court because of the cost and time involved. The main sanction against persistent non-payment, and often a very powerful one, was the threat of loss of credit-worthiness in the future.

So, contrary to the media image, licensed moneylenders did not become aggressive when people defaulted. Indeed they were fairly relaxed about it and continued to lend to people who did not manage to repay their loans in the agreed time. Moneylenders argue that as long as default is kept at a manageable or controlled level, customers should be able to retain their access to credit. But what might seem a manageable level of default to a moneylender may actually be a weekly struggle for the customer to find the repayment.

Most customers did not plan to stop using the moneylender in the foreseeable future. For about half (16), this was because they were happy using the service. For another third (11), this was because they needed the service and could not stop even if they wanted to. A few customers did expect to stop using the service some time in the future. From other research, it seems clear that some people do stop using a moneylender if they dislike the general service or have a particularly bad experience. So, generally, moneylenders do not trap unhappy customers into using them. Indeed, those who would find it most difficult to stop using the moneylender are often the very customers that the moneylender is trying to 'wean off' the service – pensioners who are finding it difficult to make repayments. These people are a cause for concern, but mainly because of their very low incomes rather than because they are being exploited by moneylenders.

The relationship between moneylenders and their customers
At a time when 'relationship banking' is generally on the decline, the weekly collected credit industry continues to rely heavily on personal contact between borrower and lender. On a personal level, relationships were very informal and friendly. Women agents in particular had close relationships with women customers. And in some respects, the moneylending industry can be thought of as part of a 'women's economy'.

Unlike its media image, the moneylending business was built on friendship rather than fear. But the opportunity existed for this friendship to be manipulated and for customers to be encouraged to borrow more than they wanted and repay more quickly than they could really afford.

The power balance within the relationship varied depending on the income level of the customer, their access to other forms of credit and their need for a loan.

The feeling of regularity and sometimes security was much more a feature of the relationship than was uncertainty or fear, as is characterised in the popular image of moneylending. Customers did not dread the weekly knock at the door, nor did they particularly look forward to it – it was simply a way of life.

1 Background to the Study

Lending money at interest has always been a controversial issue, with the earliest recorded criticisms dating back nearly 3,000 years. In the last 30 years, however, there has been a rapid growth in the availability and use of consumer credit such that the majority of people in Britain now have at least one credit commitment. Most forms of credit have lost the stigma associated with usury but the moneylending, or weekly collected credit, sector of the industry still lacks social respectability. Moneylending still carries with it the connotations previously surrounding all usury: that people are exploited by lenders charging extortionate rates of interest and using threats or actual violence.

This chapter begins with a review of the image of moneylending over the years. It then summarises the legal framework around the industry before assessing the place of moneylending in the overall credit market.

Views of moneylending

The history of Western thought is littered with criticisms of usury, by which is meant the lending of money at interest for profit. All credit comes under this definition and, for many centuries, all credit was condemned. In the 8th century BC, Aristotle saw usury as *'the most contrary to nature'* of all forms of exchange (Aristotle, 1957).

Aristotle's views became prominent again in the thirteenth century through the work of Thomas Aquinas. It was at this time that the Christian attack on usury peaked. Merely lending money was not seen as problematic but lending at interest for profit was vehemently opposed.

So usury met general disapproval in Western thought. But in Western practice, moneylending went on. This meant that borrowers had mixed feelings about lenders who were often seen as a necessary evil. Cultural images of moneylenders were very negative –

9

Shakespeare's Shylock in *The Merchant of Venice* is a classic example.

With the emergence and growth of industrialisation and capitalism, these images and attitudes to money and credit did gradually change to become more in tune with the practices of the time. Capitalist ideologues began producing their own rationalisations for making profits and using credit.

In contemporary society, credit has become even more widely accepted and used. Banks and building societies have become respectable parts of the credit industry. The condemnation of 'usury' is no longer directed at all credit but focuses on credit which is charged at *extortionate* rates of interest. The term 'moneylending' tends now to be exclusively reserved for doorstep lenders who collect payments directly from their customers, usually on a weekly basis. Although banks are technically 'moneylenders', they are seldom referred to as such. The term has almost exclusively negative connotations of credit at extortionate rates.

Another negative connotation around moneylending is that such lenders use unacceptable methods to recover repayments from people who cannot really afford to pay. At their most extreme, these methods might include violence or the threat of violence. Defenders of moneylending argue that where such bad practices exist, they are carried out by illegal moneylenders.

It is probably unwise, however, to assume that all licensed moneylenders are acting in their customers' best interests and all unlicensed operators are exploiting their customers. For example, it is unclear where informal borrowing becomes illegal moneylending. If a woman regularly lends to a number of friends, this would probably count as illegal moneylending. But to the parties involved, it is a series of informal arrangements between friends. There is evidence that, in the past at least, illegal moneylenders were people who lent money to their friends. During the first world war, a study about *'Moneylending among the London poor'* was carried out. The researchers noted that customers were often concerned about the fate of illegal moneylenders, whom they identified as, *'a poor woman who lets us have money when we need it'* (Vesselitsky and Bulkley 1917). These researchers also noted that many women used their first independent income, from wages in ammunition factories and soldiers wives' allowances to set themselves up in business as moneylenders, whether legal or not.

While there may be a general cultural view about moneylending, particularly illegal moneylending, those who experience moneylending at first hand may have a different view. As Melanie Tebbutt writes,

> In certain respects, the ethical position of the street moneylender was analogous to that of the back-street abortionist. Both originated in the desperation of the working class woman and aroused the ire of the philanthropist but the uncertain gratitude of their own community. (Tebbutt 1983)

Although general views may be different from the views of borrowers, they may still affect customers. For example, negative images may well lower expectations of lenders so that when a lender does not turn out to be violent and charge extortionate interest, then the borrower is very pleased with the service provided. It may also encourage some people to keep up repayments for fear of what might happen if they do not. So while legal moneylenders may dislike this image and worry that it might discourage some people from becoming customers, it may have some advantages for them in terms of 'policing' their existing customers.

Current views of moneylending fall into two main camps. The critical views of moneylending are most widespread and can be summed up as follows:

Critical views of moneylending

1. Doorstep collection provides an opportunity for moneylenders to pressurise their customers in two main ways. First, they may pressurise customers to borrow more money than they really want to. And second, they may use intimidation, threats or actual violence to extract payment.

2. Moneylenders charge extortionate interest rates. This is evident from the very high Annual Percentage Rates (APRs) which are charged.

3. Moneylenders are able to charge extortionate interest rates because their customers have very limited access to other forms of credit and there is little competition between moneylending companies.

4. People use moneylenders because they are in a desperate financial situation. They borrow to pay bills and so end up in a cycle of debt. Moneylenders are therefore exploiting people in vulnerable situations.

5. Moneylenders do not check ability to repay loans sufficiently and so there is a high risk of people defaulting.

6. If a customer defaults on loan repayments, extra interest or charges are added, leading to even greater debt problems.

The industry's view of the service it gives is in complete contrast to the negative picture outlined above. The CCA have laid out this view in their book, *Mirage or Reality?* (CCA UK 1992) and it can be summed up as follows:

The industry's view

1. Home collection is a vital and central aspect of the service with a number of advantages. It provides an opportunity for face-to-face assessment of ability to repay. It highlights potential or actual repayment difficulties at a very early stage, through continual contact. It is convenient, particularly for older people. It provides a routine and discipline which helps people repay their loans. Rather than being an aggressor, the collector is more of an advisor to his or her customers.

2. The APR is high because of the significant cost of home collection. The APR calculation also exaggerates the cost of short-term loans. And there are significant exemptions from the APR formula afforded to bank overdrafts – the major source of small unit cash credit.

3. Some customers do use other types of credit, particularly mail order. There is fierce competition between companies but the competitive emphasis is on having agents with the personality skills to develop good relationships with customers. Price sensitivity focuses on the amount of the weekly instalment and the total charge for credit rather than the APR. There are no barriers to entry into the market.

4. People use moneylenders for a range of reasons, but often for paying for things like holidays, decorating equipment and clothes.

Where people are getting into financial difficulties, moneylenders will discourage customers from borrowing more money.

5. Moneylenders do check ability to pay through weekly face-to-face contact with their customers. The high risk of debt is due to the financial vulnerability of the sector of the market that they operate in. This, in turn, is why other lenders, who do not use doorstep collection methods, are less likely to succeed in this sector.

6. Default interest or charges are very rarely levied. Most customers take longer to repay their loans than the agreed term. The total repayment is therefore spread over a longer period, actually producing a lower APR than is stated in the contract.

This report examines moneylenders and their customers, in the light of these existing views.

The legislative framework around moneylending

Although moneylending has a long history, its regulation by government is a much more recent development. When the power of the church declined and moneylending became more widespread, rulers were initially reluctant to interfere in what they saw as private agreements between individuals. Regulation finally came in response to increasing criticisms of lenders.

A report of the House of Commons Select Committee on Money-Lending, published in 1898, highlighted various abuses such as extortionate interest rates – 3,000 per cent in one case (See *Guide to the Consumer Credit Act*, Goode, 1994). This report led to the first Moneylenders Act in 1900 which introduced registration, though not licensing, of moneylenders. It also gave power to the courts to re-open 'harsh and unconscionable' moneylending transactions. But the absence of a licensing system meant that borrowers had to take up grievances in the civil courts, thus incurring the cost of doing so. Another problem with the Act was that it concentrated on the status of the lender rather than the nature of the transaction. Thus moneylenders were covered by the Act but banks were not.

The Moneylenders Act of 1927 introduced annual licensing and restricted the ways in which moneylenders could seek business. Canvassing cash loans became illegal. Various requirements were imposed on lenders, such as notifying a borrower in writing of a transaction. The Act gave more protection to borrowers but also led creditors to explore ways of circumventing the law through hire purchase and the sale of goods on credit, neither of which were covered by the Moneylenders Act.

The growth in instalment selling, hire purchase and other types of consumer credit was subject to a review by the Crowther Committee which recommended necessary changes in the law. The Consumer Credit Act of 1974 followed from this review and is still in operation today. Under the Act, the status of the lender becomes largely irrelevant. The law focuses more on the nature of the transaction, the amount of credit advanced and whether the borrower is an individual or partnership or corporate body. The Act divides into two main parts – one dealing with provisions relating to transactions and the other with general regulation of the consumer credit industry. Regulation of the industry takes place through licensing, restrictions on seeking business and the enforcement machinery provided by the Act. Responsibility for the Act falls on the courts, the Secretary of State for Trade and Industry, the Director General of Fair Trading and local trading standards or consumer protection officers.

Along with all other providers of consumer credit, moneylenders must have a licence – either an individual or a group one – from the Office of Fair Trading (OFT). Such a licence must now be renewed every five years. The aim of licensing is to maintain high standards of integrity and honesty among lenders. Potential licensees satisfy the OFT that they are fit to hold a licence. In forming a view, the OFT takes into account whether the applicant or any controller, employee, agent or associate of the applicant has:

- committed any offenses involving fraud or other dishonesty, or violence

- contravened any provision made under the Act

- practised discrimination

- engaged in business practices which appear to be deceitful, oppressive or otherwise unfair or improper (whether lawful or not)

About 20,000 licence applications, including renewals, are received by the OFT every year.

Broadly, the other main provisions of the Consumer Credit Act are as follows:

- The Act covers 'regulated' consumer credit agreements. These are agreements under which credit, ranging from £50 to £15,000, is provided to an individual or partnership. There are certain exemptions to this, such as low cost credit (where the APR is less than 13 per cent), normal trade credit (such as an invoice allowing a customer one month to pay) and certain categories of mortgage lending.

- Regulations prescribe the calculation of the 'total charge for credit' and the 'annual percentage rate' (APR). The total charge for credit is the overall cost to the borrower of the credit granted, including interest charges and other costs.

- The Act provides for three different categories of advertisement – 'simple', 'intermediate' and 'full' – each containing different levels of information. All 'full' adverts must give details of the APR and details of repayments (in example form if necessary). By contrast, a 'simple' advert could contain as little as the lenders name. The aim of these regulations is to ensure that advertising provides useful information and does not mislead.

- In broad terms, it is an offence to canvas cash loans off trade premises unless responding to a written request from a potential borrower.

- In the agreement they sign, consumers must be given basic information about the terms and conditions of the transaction. Certain prescribed forms of statements, for example, on cancellation and termination rights, must be included. The consumer must be given a copy of the agreement.

- For certain agreements signed away from trade premises, the borrower has a right to cancel.

- The Act gives borrowers the right to terminate credit agreements ahead of time and the right to receive a rebate of charges when doing so. Certain formulae for working out rebates are prescribed.

The report from the Crowther Committee in 1971 had warned of a level of credit costs *'above which it becomes socially harmful to make loans available'* and as a result the Consumer Credit Act gave the courts power to overturn 'extortionate credit bargains'. But over the years few cases came to court. In November 1990 – at the Government's request – the OFT began a review of those sections of the Consumer Credit Act which dealt with 'extortionate credit bargains'. These provisions are concerned not only with the *costs* of credit, but also with other practices which *'grossly contravene the ordinary principles of fair trading'*.

The OFT review argued that the Consumer Credit Act had not dealt adequately with the problems of socially harmful loans. It argued that whilst *'high APRs alone do not necessarily indicate socially harmful lending'*, nevertheless in some cases, the costs of credit were oppressive or extortionate due to the breakdown of competition. This particularly affected people on low incomes who had limited choice of lenders. Top-up loans were also cited as problematic. These are where borrowers who already have one loan, clear the outstanding balance using money from a second loan, and are thereby locked into a cycle of increasing debt, with the process being continually repeated. Early settlement rebates are often not given. The OFT review also identified as unacceptable a series of practices found with both secured and unsecured lending, which included, for example, high-pressure selling.

Broadly, the OFT made two recommendations as a result of this review. It suggested that the terminology of the Act which defined unacceptable levels of charge should be relaxed. This would make it easier for debtors to challenge the rates they were charged. Secondly, it recommended that the test for establishing whether other practices were unacceptable should be brought into line with the 'fitness' test for licensing. In other words, whether the practice involved any behaviour which is *'deceitful or oppressive'* (OFT 1991). This points directly to the relationship between a borrower and lender. But it still leaves the courts with a fair amount of latitude over whether a transaction is unjust.

Through 1993 and into 1994, as part of the Government's Deregulation Initiative, the OFT consulted on the possibility of relaxing the regulation of lenders under the Consumer Credit Act. It believed that some regulations, *'impose costs and burdens on the providers of credit that go beyond what is necessary for effective consumer protection'*. In its consultation document, the OFT argued that *'licensing remains an effective weapon against unscrupulous traders'* (OFT 1993). But other regulations in the Act are open to discussion, for example those relating to advertising, written quotations, the calculation of APRs, copy documents, calculation notices and early settlement. The OFT has recently released its review of these issues (OFT 1994). There are two main implications for moneylending. Firstly it is suggested that the lower limit of loans which are covered by the Consumer Credit Act be raised from £50 to £150. Secondly, it is proposed that APRs need not be given for credit deals under £150. The CCA have told us that their recommendation to their members would be to continue making full APR disclosure even if these suggestions were to become law, although they do welcome – and agree with – the thinking behind the proposals.

The place of moneylending in the overall credit market
The 1980s saw a boom in the use of consumer credit, following deregulation which eased restrictions on both lenders and borrowers. By the early 1990s there was a wide range of possible sources of credit besides the doorstep moneylender. They included bank overdrafts, loans from banks, building societies and finance houses, credit and store cards, hire purchase and credit sale, mail order catalogues, credit unions and the social fund.

Previous research has shown that household income was *not* important in determining whether a household entered the credit market. Low-income families were just as likely to have credit commitments as those who were better-off. They did, however, differ significantly in the types of credit they used and their reasons for borrowing (Berthoud and Kempson 1992).

For high-income households, credit promoted a consumer lifestyle, buying goods like cars and consumer durables. In low-income households, credit was more often used to deal with financial hardship, to pay bills and other commitments or to buy essential items such as clothing and basic household goods and furniture, often in an emergency.

Better-off families had many revolving credit facilities, including overdraft agreements, credit charge and store cards, some of which may not have been used for credit. Worse-off families were more restricted in their access to credit and mostly relied on mail order catalogues or borrowed informally from family members or friends.

Some commercial credit sources – banks, building societies and specialist retailers – dealt mainly in large advances to prosperous customers. Others – check traders, moneylenders and pawn brokers – occupied a niche market, lending modest amounts to poor families.

Taking this analysis together, credit sources could be aggregated into three groups depending on the average income of their customers.

Up-market sources included credit cards, authorised overdrafts, and bank and building society loans; mid-market credit was largely hire purchase agreements and finance house loans but also included credit unions, while down-market credit included not only moneylending but pawn broking and the social fund (Berthoud and Kempson 1992).

A recent study, which interviewed 74 low-income families in depth gave more information about the extent of market segmentation. This suggested that there were two credit markets, even among low-income families. People who worked full-time, even in low-paid jobs, tended to use up- and mid-market credit; while those without an earned income tended to use the down-market sources like moneylenders, pawn brokers, buying 'on tick' and the social fund. Mail order catalogues were used widely by families and cut across these divisions. This showed that, at least for low-income families with children, the main competitors for moneylenders were the social fund and mail order firms. Credit unions had made no significant impact on poor families despite their availability to about half of the people interviewed (Kempson et al 1994).

There have been very few studies which have looked specifically at moneylending. But the PSI study of credit use among 74 low-income families with children did contain some interesting information about moneylending. Just over a third (28) of these families had used moneylenders at one time or another and about a fifth (16) were current users.

This is an interesting study because it gives information on current customers, ex-customers and people from similar backgrounds who have never been customers. But it is limited to low-income families with children and these may be a minority of all moneylender customers.

The study showed that current customers included a disproportionate number of couples with children rather than lone parents, and a disproportionate number of non-workers. There was very little overlap between these families and those who used other forms of credit, with the exception of mail order and the social fund. The attractions of moneylending were said by customers to be the flexibility of repayment schedules, the convenience of doorstep collection, familiarity with the system and the ease of access to credit. The drawbacks were that it was too easy to become dependent on this source of credit and collectors could be pushy. High interest was also seen as a major disadvantage.

The 12 ex-customers stopped using moneylending for a variety of reasons which are detailed in later sections of this book. For example, they thought the interest was too high and that the goods they bought on credit from moneylenders were low quality and expensive.

Some people from similar backgrounds were not and never had been customers of moneylenders. In some cases, their non-use was part of a general objection to using any forms of credit but in others, it was related to the high interest charged and the fear of what might happen if they got involved with such lenders. The image of the loanshark certainly deterred people from becoming customers. As one respondent said,

> *... and these loan people what you hear a lot about, I think they're a bit rough ... Well, I've heard of people who lend money if they don't give it back in a certain time they blow the kneecaps off and that.*

There were, however, no concrete examples of such 'strong-arm' tactics. Hearsay, or the mass media, were the main sources of evidence for these views. This is not to say that such tactics are not used, just that people did not have direct experience of them.

Another fairly recent study which focused on moneylending was carried out in Ireland among moneylending customers who had contacted welfare agencies because of problems with debt (Daly and Walsh 1988). Ninety-nine people were interviewed, the vast majority of whom were families with children living long-term on social welfare benefits. The study identified the root of these people's problems as income inadequacy rather than their use of moneylenders. But the report did comment that the costs of this type of credit were very high and that the moneylenders operated without scrutiny. The respondents gave details of their experiences with moneylenders, some of whom were unlicensed. But a licence did not necessarily guarantee satisfactory treatment. About a third of respondents said that they had been frightened by their moneylender but most of these said that it was a general feeling rather than the result of a specific experience.

This study is interesting but is limited in that the sample is only drawn from those who have had problems with moneylenders and have visited welfare agencies. These may be a-typical of all customers.

A much earlier study of moneylending involved detailed interviews with *'fairly respectable'* people in the district of Limehouse. Although the study is now very old, it is remarkable how much similarity there is between its findings and the current studies. Out of the first 100 women visited in Limehouse, 47 said that they were current or previous customers of a moneylender. A further 32 said that they did not borrow but that they did pawn their belongings on occasion. Many of the moneylenders were themselves women, either working informally for themselves or as agents of loan companies (Vesselitsky and Bulkley 1917).

Virtually all of the customers were married people. This is because widows, especially those with children, were considered too poor to lend to. As the authors remarked,

> *It is not apparently that widows do not try to borrow, but theirs is usually the hopeless poverty on which the most enterprising moneylender is not willing to hazard her savings.*

People borrowed from a moneylender for various reasons. A few borrowed to provide investment capital for a business venture. But most borrowed to meet the current expenses of the household. Once people started using a moneylender, they rarely stopped and this did cause hardship for some customers. Threats, abuse and bullying were used on occasion to extract payment. The authors concluded with a remark which might still be made today when they stated that moneylending was,

> *... one more example of the high prices the poor have to pay for everything in proportion to their poverty.*

The research methods used in the study
The main aim of this study was to investigate and understand the nature of the relationship between customers and collectors. This was achieved through conducting detailed interviews with a small number of collectors and customers and directly observing moneylenders on their rounds. But since the study would only directly involve a small number of people, it was thought wise to interview directors and managers from each of the six companies included in the study so that we could gain an overview of the industry as well as information on our specific case studies.

From previous knowledge of the industry, we knew that the best way of obtaining access to the companies was to enlist the support of their trade association, CCA UK. After some discussion, CCA agreed to cooperate.

In order for us to select the sample, CCA sent us its full membership list. The list gave details of the size of the company including the number of employees, the nature of the company's business – whether cash loans, goods or vouchers, and the geographical location of the company.

The researchers chose two of the large companies from the list of five giants and these agreed to take part in the research. CCA made the first contact with these companies, asking them if they would take part in the research. Both agreed.

The researchers then selected about ten medium-sized companies. These were given to CCA who were instructed to start with companies at the top of the list and work down it until they were able to gain agreement from two companies. A similar process occurred with the small companies. The reason for oversampling the small and medium-sized companies was that the fieldwork had to be conducted at a very particular time to fit in with the researcher's other commitments and so CCA had to arrange the details very quickly.

The six companies were selected to reflect the different types of company in the industry in terms of size, type of business and geographical location.

Having selected the six companies, it was then possible to select the eight collectors. In the small companies, the managers were also the collectors of the company and so there was no second selection process. In the medium-sized and large companies, the researcher specified which area they wished to work in. For example, we might have specified that we wanted to include a collector who worked in Clapham. This meant that the company had very little opportunity to direct us to particular collectors as there would be few collectors who worked in these areas. The researcher selected the areas to reflect a range of socio-geographic factors – for example, inner city, suburb, small town. Practical factors were also important since the fieldwork involved fairly long periods in the North, Midlands and South.

The collectors sampled reflected a mix in terms of sex, age, experience, locality of work, hours of work and employment status.

Having selected the eight collectors, the 31 customers were selected after the observation work. This enabled the researcher to select a reasonably representative number in terms of demographic factors and the different customer types. For example, people were selected to reflect the fact that some customers always paid the full repayment every week, some missed and some paid reduced amounts every week.

The observation work with each collector involved visiting the local office and accompanying the collector on their weekly rounds. About 500 customers were observed in their weekly dealings with their collector. During this time, customers were given a letter about the study.

All of the observation work and interviews were conducted personally by the author.

Further details of the methods used are given in an appendix.

The fieldwork produced data at four levels – company level, manager level, collector level and customer level. Table 1 gives a summary of the information collected.

Table 1   **Details of the companies, collectors and customers who took part in the study**

Company	Collector		Number of customers interviewed
A - LARGE	Woman	South	4
	Woman	North	4
B - SMALL	Man	North	2
C - MEDIUM	Man	Midlands	5
D - LARGE	Woman	Midlands	4
	Man	South	5
E - SMALL	Man	South	4
F - MEDIUM	Man	South	3

The terminology and structure of the report

For the purposes of this report, the term moneylending, or weekly collected credit, is used to refer to credit which involves relatively small loans, say from £30 to £1,000, without security and for a fixed period. It is usually paid in weekly instalments and the interest rate is set at the start. The loan may be for cash or for a variety of items such as bedding, electrical goods, clothes and gift vouchers. The instalments are usually collected personally by someone who calls on the customer each week or month.

Throughout this report, the term 'moneylending' is used to describe the type of credit outlined above. The industry itself uses the phrase 'weekly collected credit'. While the industry's phrase has fewer of the negative cultural connotations outlined earlier, most of those outside the industry will have little idea about what is meant by it. This report uses the term 'moneylending' rather than 'weekly collected credit' partly because it is a much better known term and partly because the very aim of the study was to see whether the connotations surrounding this term are justified.

At this point, it is also worth mentioning the different terms used for the people who actually work collecting and lending money from door-to-door. The larger companies almost exclusively call them 'agents'. But one of the managing directors of a medium-sized company referred to his staff as 'reps'. A more old-fashioned term which is rarely used nowadays is 'travellers'.

Some companies and some customers talked about their 'collectors'. Other customers referred to their 'callers', or very occasionally, their 'tallymen'. A few called them 'Scotch drapers' as there was a tendency for Scottish men to migrate South of the border and set up business selling clothing on credit.

Most customers simply used their collector's first name when speaking to or about them. No-one in the industry, including the customers, talked about 'moneylenders'. In this report, the term 'moneylender' is sometimes used because it is the most generally recognised term but it should be remembered that such a term has the cultural connotations referred to earlier. It is also important to remember the dual functions of lending and collecting, which are slightly obscured by the term 'moneylender'. So the report also uses the term '*collector*' when the emphasis is on that side of the business. And it uses the terms '*agent*' when referring to the people who worked for the larger companies and '*owner-collector*' to describe people who ran their own businesses.

The report begins by looking at the moneylending companies and the people who actually lend and collect from door-to-door. It then focuses on the customers and examines how, why and what type of people become customers. Each chapter ends with some key points. The report finishes with some conclusions and policy implications.

KEY POINTS

- Cultural views of moneylending are extremely negative and stem from early religious criticisms of charging any interest on loans.

- The main legislative framework around moneylending is contained in the 1974 Consumer Credit Act. The Government is currently reviewing the regulation of lenders under the Act with a view to possible deregulation.

- Although credit use is just as common among low-income groups as high-income groups, those on a low income are much more likely to use certain types of credit such as moneylending, mail order and loans from the social fund.

- 6 companies were included in this study. From within these companies, 8 moneylenders and 31 customers were interviewed. These 8 moneylenders were also observed on their rounds.

---

2 The Moneylenders

The moneylending industry in Britain today is a big business. In 1993, the weekly collected credit arm of the Provident Financial Services group of companies, which is the largest company in the sector, had a turnover of £249 million and pre-tax profits of £55.1 million. This chapter begins by looking at the size and nature of the moneylending companies. It then explores how, why and what types of people actually lend and collect money week-on-week from door-to-door.

Moneylending companies
There are currently about 1200 licensed moneylending companies in the UK today. These break down into the following:

- six national companies, each of which employ at least 1,000 agents

- 50-60 medium-sized regional companies, which employ 50-100 agents each

- 700 small companies, which employ an average of 10 agents each

- 400 sole or very small traders, perhaps with one employee

Nearly 800 of these companies belong to the Consumer Credit Association of the United Kingdom (CCA), the main trade association for weekly collected credit companies. The CCA includes 5 of the 6 national companies, 40-50 of the medium-sized ones, 300 of the small companies and the majority of the sole or very small traders.

Of course, there is also the illegal, unlicensed moneylending industry, the size of which is completely unknown. Although the illegal sector attracts most interest, anecdotal evidence suggests that it operates on a relatively small scale nationally. But it might assume great importance in very localised poor areas.

By far the largest company in the licensed industry, and probably the most well known, is Provident. The original company was founded in 1880 by a non-conformist philanthropist who wanted to help poor people buy shoes and clothing for their children. His invention was check trading – a system of buying 'checks' on credit which could then be used to purchase various items. Today the Provident businesses have about 9,000 agents – well over two-thirds of whom are women. Those agents deal with about 1.1 million customers. The combined turnover of the Provident credit businesses in 1993 was £249 million.

London Scottish, Morses, Shopacheck and S&U stores are also major national companies, as is Greenwoods, which is one of the Provident businesses mentioned above. S&U stores is the one large company which is not a member of the CCA.

These six large companies have various tiers of management. A line manager directly oversees the work of the agent and will spend time on the rounds. They will cover for agents when they are on holiday or off sick, visit new customers and make calls to some customers who have fallen into arrears. The line manager will be responsible for, perhaps, 10 agents. Above the line manager is a branch or area manager. Above that tier of management there is sometimes another tier of regional management before we reach head office.

Two of these five large companies were involved in the research.

There are, nationally, about 50-60 medium-sized companies which tend to operate in a particular region of the country. The two medium-sized regional companies which took part in this research are typical of this sector of the industry.

Both were established between the two world wars by working-class men. One of the firms was established by a man who started by lending informally to people before going into business as a credit draper. Now, the business had moved over to cash loans, with goods accounting for only about 10 per cent of business. The managers found it difficult to give a figure for company turnover but said that their cash flow was about £5 million a year and that the 40 or so agents who worked for them collected a total of about £85,000 a week (that is, just over £2,000 per agent).

The managing director of the other medium sized company referred to his collectors as 'reps' of which there were 10 currently working for the company. The 10 of them were collecting about £30,000 a week overall. Most of this company's business was in cash loans but about 20 per cent was in goods. Although there were only

10 reps working for the company, their rounds were widely spread in geographical terms and so they were more akin to a regional company than the smaller companies.

Finally, there are a large number of small companies and sole traders, lending cash to a fairly localised community. Despite their relatively large numbers, they account for a very small proportion of both customers and collectors. Again the two small companies that took part in the research illustrate this sector of the industry.

One of these small companies was a family business which had its origins between the two world wars when relatives of the current owner had set themselves up as credit drapers. As with many of the companies mentioned so far, the rise of mail order and the retail boom from the 1960s onwards meant that there was less need for retail credit from the traditional tallyman or credit draper. Today, goods only formed about 10 per cent of this small company's business. The current owner had a collection round which he himself looked after. He only employed one other collector but there was a clerical assistant and his father still helped out when necessary.

The other small company was a sole trader. He had started in the business in the 1980s offering cash loans. He had taken over some customers from a friend whom he knew in the trade and then built the round up from there. Like many in the business, he found it difficult to say what his earnings were. He had a £5,000 overdraft and just took money out of the business as and when required. His style of living was comfortable but not excessively so.

The product

Most companies in the industry deal mainly in cash loans but some also sell a variety of products, from shopping vouchers to goods such as bedding, clothes and electrical equipment which can be bought on credit. Some companies also provide other services such as renting out coin-in-the-slot TVs and hampers which are paid for in advance of Christmas rather than on credit. One of the larger companies, Morse's, deals only in insurance sales and selling goods on credit.

In the past, many companies sold trading checks which could be supplied on credit and then could only be used in certain shops with which the moneylending company had an arrangement. The trading check now seems to be a thing of the past, replaced in part by vouchers from major chain stores which are exactly the same as the gift vouchers they sell themselves. For example, people can buy goods from Argos using vouchers bought on credit through the moneylender rather than buying the vouchers straight from the shop. And they can use them in the shop without anyone knowing how or where they were acquired. Some types of vouchers can be used in a range of stores.

Companies generally offer people different sizes and lengths of loan. These are often laid out in ready-reckoner tables that agents keep with them on the rounds. Few companies will offer loans – for cash, vouchers or goods – over less than 14 weeks. Some companies will offer loans for up to 120 weeks. The amount which people can borrow varies from £10 to £1,500. Smaller amounts are usually borrowed over shorter time periods.

There is a higher amount of interest on cash loans compared with goods or vouchers. This is because companies receive some financial incentive from chain stores to sell their vouchers, in much the same way as Access and Visa are paid a commission by retailers. In the case of goods, part or all of the credit charge can be assimilated within the mark-up on those goods.

The costs of credit

The Annual Percentage Rate (APR) is probably one of the biggest bones of contention about moneylending. The APR was originally devised to give consumers a way of comparing the costs of different types of credit. Critics of moneylending argue that the APRs are extortionate. They would also argue that companies can only succeed in charging these rates because people have no alternative source of credit. The industry argues that the calculation of the APR exaggerates the cost of short-term loans. Furthermore it argues that it must include the costs of doorstep collection in its APRs, so that the pure interest component is much lower than it would seem from the overall APR figure. It is also claimed that many customers repay their loan over a longer period than the original agreement. No extra charges are incurred so the actual APR is lower than the contractually-stated figure. The industry also points out that the fixed costs incurred by any lender tend to make small loans a more expensive proposition.

Table 2 gives some examples of the types of loans granted by three of the companies that took part in the study. Company A was a small company whereas companies B and C were larger companies.

Table 2   Typical cash loans provided by moneylending companies

Company	Length of loan in weeks	Amount of loan	Charge for credit	Total amount payable	Weekly payment	APR (%)
A	16	£60	£12	£72	£4.50	215
B	20	£60	£24	£84	£4.20	481
C	20	£200	£60	£260	£13	354
B	50	£200	£140	£340	£6.80	230
C	52	£500	£279.50	£779.50	£15*	168
B	100	£500	£500	£1,000	£10	127
C	104	£800	£698.40	£1,498.40	£14.40**	105

*   The first payment will be £14.50. Thereafter, £15.

**   The first payment will be £15.20. Thereafter, £14.40

In this sample, the smaller companies tended to make smaller loans for much shorter periods. Yet despite this, they had lower APRs than the larger companies. So, for example, the 16 week loan shown above is from a small company and has an APR of 215 per cent. The shortest loan from one of the large companies is for 20 weeks with an APR of 481 per cent for the same £60 loan.

Information from the CCA about the sector as a whole suggests that while some smaller companies charge less than majors, in general, small firms' charges are broadly in line with larger companies.

It might at first seem strange that some smaller companies provide cheaper loans but, unlike the larger companies, they do not have various tiers of managers and administrators, most of whom do not collect from door-to-door and so constitute overheads. However, the larger companies are borrowing larger sums of money from banks which they, in turn, lend out. And so they may be able to borrow this money at lower rates of interest than the smaller companies. And smaller companies are generally lending smaller sums which do tend, as has already been argued, to cost more than larger loans.

Our research showed that the larger companies offered much greater flexibility in terms of the length and size of loans they offered. The smallest and shortest loan from one of the larger companies was

Table 3   Comparison of loan from a building society with loan from a moneylender

Length of loan	Amount of loan	Charge for credit	Total amount payable	Monthly payment	APR (%)
Building society					
52 weeks	£500	£94.96	£594.96	£49.58	22
Moneylender					
52 weeks	£500	£279.50	£779.50	£64.95	168

£50 over 20 weeks, the largest and longest from the same company was £1500 over 100 weeks.

The APR was fixed according to the length of loan rather than the amount lent. Within each company, the APR was lower if someone took out a loan over a longer period. For example, in one company, any loan over 20 weeks incurred an APR of 354 per cent compared with 230 per cent if it was taken out over 50 weeks. So the longer loans were cheaper in terms of APR.

Although there are some limitations to the APR as a measure for comparing the costs of different types of credit, it is the best measure available. But people do not always use the APR and may resort to other more immediately obvious ways of comparing two loans. For example, they may look at the amount - as a proportion of the principal - which is being paid back in interest. In the table shown above, it is cheaper, according to the APR, to borrow £500 over 100 weeks from company B than over 52 weeks from company C. But company B will be paid back the principal amount plus another 100 per cent of the principal amount. Whereas company C only want the principal amount plus just over 55 per cent of the principal amount. This is not a good way of comparing the cost of credit but it is probable that people see interest simply in terms of the extra amount they have to pay on top of the principal amount rather than in terms of the APR.

Table 3 gives details of a loan which could be taken out from a building society. The smallest amount such organisations tend to lend is £500 which has to be repaid over a year in monthly instalments. As we can see, the APR is substantially lower than a similar loan from a moneylending company.

The APR is 22 per cent compared with 168 per cent for a comparable loan from a moneylender. And the charge for credit from the moneylender (£279.50) is three times that of the charge from the building society (£94.96). Of course, other types of credit, such as an authorised bank overdraft, may not be as cheap as a building society loan, but all in all, moneylending is much more expensive than other forms of credit.

Moneylending agents

So far in this chapter we have looked at the moneylending companies but customers generally know little about these companies. Their experience is with the people who call at their door to lend money and collect repayments. There is no accurate data about the number of these callers or the type of people they are. From discussions with representatives of the industry, our best estimate is that there are 27,000 licensed moneylenders. The majority of these moneylenders are women, working for the six national companies.

There are two types of people who lend and collect money from door-to-door. The vast majority are *agents* working for companies. Six of these were included in the study. Others run their own firms, having started, taken over or inherited a moneylending company. Two of these were included in the study. This section of the chapter concentrates on moneylending agents.

When a company was looking for a new agent, they were looking for someone who would be able both to lend and collect as much money as possible. Someone who was good at selling goods, vouchers or cash was not very useful to the company if they could not collect the repayments. And someone who was good at collecting would only be successful in the short-term unless they could also sell. But what sorts of people were considered to be good at this kind of work?

The companies had slightly different philosophies about which type of people made the best agents. Some were looking for people from the same social class background as their customers. Others were looking for people with slightly more upwardly-aspiring and achieving backgrounds. Some companies preferred women to men as agents. All companies agreed that maturity was important in an agent although they had different ideas about the age at which such maturity was achieved.

The six agents interviewed as part of the study generally reflected the philosophies of the companies they worked for.

Social class

One of the large companies felt that it was important for an agent to come from a very similar background to their customers. Of course, their customers came from a range of backgrounds, but a fairly narrow range nevertheless. Most customers were from working-class backgrounds – people in manual or routine non-manual work, pensioners, unemployed people and lone parents. Many were living in council accommodation. The company felt that an agent from the same background would be more easily accepted and more readily trusted by the customer if they were 'one of us'. The agent would be able to empathise with their customers and draw on shared experience and knowledge.

This company was happy to encourage existing customers or friends of agents to become agents themselves. And it had a policy of encouraging, almost to the point of requiring, agents to be customers at the same time as being agents, even if this only meant buying a hamper once a year. This meant that the lines between being a customer and being an agent were deliberately blurred.

The two agents who worked for this company reflected its staff recruitment philosophy. Both came from working-class backgrounds. One was a woman in her late 30s who was married to a manual worker. She had previously worked in various part-time jobs in the service sector. She had been a customer of the company at one time and then was good friends with another agent who introduced her to the work.

The other agent was in her early 40s and was also married to a manual worker. Both of her sons were unemployed. A friend of hers was an agent of the company and had recommended her for a job. This agent said of her customers,

> *I always say 'never think they're any different from me'*

This quote is interesting since, by talking about 'them' and 'me', the agent is consciously seeing herself apart from the customers while trying to minimise that distance.

Other companies and managers agreed that it was important for agents to get on well with their customers. But they did not agree that the agent should come from the same social class. As a senior manager of one company said,

> We try to recruit from the middle-class people where the agent is looking for a supplementary income for luxury purchases rather than necessities like paying the gas bill, electricity bill. We do that because we hope that the agent is capable of having a meaningful conversation with the customer. We feel that if they are neighbours of existing customers they will perhaps not have the right sort of development with that customer.... Where many of our competitors say that a good agent would be someone who is living amongst our customers, is probably one of our customers and therefore relates to them and thinks in the way they do, we would say that's not necessarily the route. You want somebody that's a bit brighter, a bit more perceptive.

This manager was concerned that if an agent came from the very same background, they might identify too closely with the customer, to the detriment of the company. Agents who got too involved with their customers might make bad business decisions. For example, if an agent had built up a close relationship with someone who was in urgent need of money, they might lend it to them even though the customer had little chance of paying it back on time. Also, an agent may not try quite so hard to encourage repayments from someone they were very friendly with. As a senior manager explained,

> If you get too close then you can't refuse credit can you? You grant credit from the heart rather than the head and that doesn't do the customer any good either because the customer becomes over-indebted, can't afford to pay you and so you eventually lose them as a customer. If you strike the right balance that they can afford to pay, they will continue to deal with you for a long time to come. But it's a fine balance between the two.

There was another reason for not recruiting people who needed income for *'necessities like paying the gas bill'*. This was the fear that some agents would themselves be in such need of money, that they might defraud the company. Managers played down this fear, saying that such fraud was unusual. Nevertheless, one of the larger companies had an internal audit department, one of whose key tasks was to monitor agents for fraud. One type of fraud was where an agent would pretend to lend out money either to existing customers or fictitious new customers. Some repayments would be made but then the agent would disappear with the money. One of the customers interviewed in the study had been a victim of this type of fraud. A previous agent had claimed that she had bought some goods, which the agent had actually kept for herself.

The agents of these other companies reflected the views of their managers that their agents should not be too similar to their customers. One had always worked in offices until she managed her own shop. Her husband was self-employed in the financial sector. Their income was relatively unstable but both were keen to improve their living standards. This woman felt that she was different from many of her customers. Sometimes her customers pointed this out and it was a potential source of friction between them. She explained one recent incident,

> *A few weeks ago I had my son's car. Now I don't think it's posh, it's only a D reg, but it's a white Metro ... but this woman says, 'you come in your flashy mod cars!' and I said, 'it's my son's', 'how can your son afford a car like that?' so I said, 'what the hell's it got to do with you?' But then again my lad goes to work and why shouldn't he have what he wants?*

It was not uncommon for agents who were from slightly different backgrounds from their customers to be scathing of customers who seemed either to have no intention of working or were working and claiming benefits at the same time. One agent said that these people often criticised her for her relatively affluent lifestyle. Customers had made comments about the smart clothes she wore and the holidays she had been on. The implication was always that she could not understand the financial difficulties they had. Although she had a great deal of sympathy for many of her customers she did explain some of their financial misfortune on a lack of work ethic or bad money management. So she was much more detached from her customers than the two agents mentioned earlier. In some cases this did lead to friction between her and her customers but it also meant that she was able to see things from the company's point of view.

One of the characteristics of some agents, which often set them apart from their customers, was that they had an entrepreneurial spirit. One of the agents who worked for a medium-sized company certainly saw himself in this light. He was in his mid 50s and had spent a few years in manual work before breaking free from the chains of an employer, as he saw it, to work for himself. He took a similar attitude to the female agent mentioned above: if he could make a decent living through hard work, so could, and should, everyone else. But he tried to make the difference between himself and his customers less obvious. He wore a tie when on his rounds, but his trousers were fairly casual and he had a bomber jacket. He prided himself on having the 'gift-of-the-gab' and being able to get on with anyone. He saw himself as hard-working and down-to-earth.

The other two agents were even more detached from their customers. One was in his mid 70s. He had worked in a shop before going into this business. Although his social class background was different from his customers, the more apparent difference was in terms of ethnicity. He was white, as were all the other collectors interviewed in the study. But many, if not most, of his customers were Afro-Caribbean. The combination of his age and his ethnicity meant that he was also much more detached from his customers than other agents. But the extent of the differences between himself and his customers did not lead him to be critical of his customers. He was not quick to condemn poor money management or lack of work ethic as some other agents were. Indeed, he talked warmly about his customers and had a great deal of respect for them.

The last of the six agents had a similar approach. He was in his mid 60s and had left school at 14. After various jobs he started work as an agent and had been in the job ever since, although for different companies. He was fairly relaxed with his customers and seemed neither too close nor too detached. Unlike some of the other agents, he had not really thought about whether he was like or unlike his customers. As he said, he was,

> *Friendly, but never too friendly! I always try to be relaxed and casual with them.*

This reflects the view that agents should be close to customers while retaining a degree of detachment and ability to see things from the company's perspective.

Although some of the agents were also customers of their companies at the same time, one was adamant that they would never be a customer of their own company,

> *I wouldn't come to a company like this, me, I'd go to the bank. I've bought things off [the company] but I pay cash. I wouldn't dream of paying these interest rates. I mean I'm selling it to everybody else, but would you go to a company like us?*

This quote illustrates the gulf between the collector and their customers. But the fact that the agent mentioned doubts about the business show that there was also some detachment from the company.

Sex and age

There was slight disagreement between managers about whether men or women made better agents. Most agents in the largest companies are women. This is partly because of the conditions of work but also because the companies are keen on recruiting women.

No manager said that men were better than women as agents. The disagreement came between those who said that women were better than men and those who said that sex made no difference. Those who argued that women made better agents said that women found it easier to get on with people. Most customers were women and so there was an immediate common ground of experience. Partly because of this, some managers thought that women agents were better at encouraging customers to buy or repay. As one of the few female managers said,

I think a woman can be a little bit cheekier and people accept it off a woman more so than they accept it off a man. You can go 'come on Mrs so-and-so' you know, whereas men don't tend to do that.

Other managers thought that personality was more important than sex and that some men could get on with customers just as well as women. But processes of socialisation often mean that personality characteristics are related to structural ones, such as sex and age.

All managers considered maturity to be very important in an agent. Once again, this was because older people were considered better at establishing good personal relationships. But maturity was also important because maturer people were usually more reliable and responsible than their younger counterparts. Reliability and responsibility were thought to be crucial in the business as someone had to do the round week in, week out. According to managers, younger people did not seem to appreciate this and tended to take more time off. And not only did the round have to be done every week, it had to be done in a very particular way. For example, Mrs X might have to be visited at exactly 2.35 on a Thursday otherwise she would not be in and she would miss that weekly payment. Reliability and responsibility were also related to fears over fraud. Older people were thought to be more honest and trustworthy.

A woman in her late thirties with young children was considered ideal by many managers. But one manager went for people older than this,

> *I wouldn't take anyone on really under 50 ... In the past I have taken on some 19 year-olds and they've both let me down, really let me down, you know. I'd get a phone call on a Monday from one of their mothers, 'he's got a dental appointment' and things like that.*

The ages of the collectors who took part in the study varied from the late 30s to mid 70s and so satisfied the companies' requirement of being 'mature'.

The three women agents were younger than the three male agents interviewed. They had all started working as agents when their children had been at school and had been in the job for an average of about 8 years. Most of them had been in various jobs previous to becoming an agent but saw this job as a convenient way of earning relatively good money. Their husbands were employed but had experienced unemployment at various times. All three worked for large companies.

The male agents were not only older than the women but had also been in the business longer. They had all had jobs in other fields but had been agents for about 30 years on average. They worked longer hours than the women. They were all married and had adult children. Their jobs had brought in the main wage when their children had been young.

Personality

Managers stressed various personality traits which were often linked to sex, age and social class. The ability to relate to customers was the most important requirement in an agent. As one manager said,

> *I think it mainly all comes back down to personality ... bright and cheerful, so when you knock on the door you pass it on to the customers. If your face is down they soon catch on and it's strange, they don't seem to want to know people like that, they want happy-go-lucky.*

Managers also stressed that it was important for agents to be able to get on with anyone and not pre-judge people according to how they lived. In the words of a second manager,

You can't just look at an agent and think she's going to make a good agent. Confidence with people is important and being able to walk into anyone's house, whether it be the palace or the pits. That customer, whether they're absolutely filthy, he's a good customer.

Honesty and reliability were also important and similarly linked with social class and age, in the minds of managers.

Types of agent
Taking all of this together, there were two main types of agent:
- *one of us* - these moneylenders were from a very similar background to their customers. They were generally women in their 30s or 40s. They found it easy to empathise with their customers.

- *entrepreneurs* - these moneylenders came from a slightly higher social class or had moved away from their working class roots. Some of these were judgemental about their customers' poor money management or lack of work ethic. They were more detached from their customers than other agents.

Becoming an agent
The reasons why people became agents
Managers may look for certain types of people when they are recruiting, but what motivates people to apply for a job as an agent? There were four main reasons why agents had initially been attracted to the work - convenience of hours, pay, self-employment and the social aspects of the work

The convenience of the working hours had particularly motivated the female agents to apply for jobs. Agents tended to work two to four days a week. This enabled women to combine the job with looking after their homes and families. And although the hours of the round did reflect the hours which were convenient for customers, there was some scope for the collector to arrange collections at suitable times for them. Some women tried to arrange their rounds so that they could pick their children up from school. The job was also convenient for mothers because during the school holidays they could take their children on the round in their car and so could keep their jobs going.

Most of the agents, particularly the women who only wanted part-time jobs, could only expect to get relatively low-paid jobs if they were not moneylending agents. Some had previously worked as cleaners, waitresses and shop assistants with rates of pay which were often around £3-4 an hour. The rates of pay that they could earn from moneylending were significantly higher than this. One agent had worked out, with the help of her accountant, that she was taking home an average of about £7 an hour.

The male agents were slightly less attracted by the rate of pay but it was considered a decent amount to live on and provided enough for themselves and their families. The main aspect of the pay which motivated the men was that it reflected the amount of effort put into the job.

Many of the collectors were attracted by the self-employed nature of the work. This was particularly true of those agents who were the more entrepreneurial, upwardly-aspiring and achieving members of the working class. They were attracted to commission-based work because it seemed to provide the opportunity to reward according to ability and effort.

Being out-and-about also meant that there was no supervisor watching over them and so there was more independence and responsibility. Agents were virtually their own boss. As one agent put it,

> *There's nobody chasing you up. You're on your own all day long ... It's great in the summer, you're walking about in the sun. I still don't mind it in the winter as long as you're wrapped up. You've got nobody harassing you, no bosses about.*

As well as paying on commission, companies also ran various competitions to encourage sales. For example, bonuses were given to the agent who sold the most goods during a sales promotion. This appealed to the entrepreneurial spirit of the agents who were keen to do their best.

Given that companies were recruiting people they considered out-going and friendly, it is not surprising that collectors were also attracted to the social aspects of their work. One female agent highlighted this as one of the main attractions,

> *You're a bit of a social worker and everything in this game. Everybody tells you their problems. I mean not all the people are nice but I would say 90 per cent of the people you deal with are very nice.*

A male agent also considered himself a 'people person',

> *I had other little jobs but mainly I always worked dealing with people and I'm the type of person who comes across to people. I can get on*

with most people, probably 98 out of 100 would take to me because I'm just ordinary. I'm not rough and ready. I don't act, I don't try to put on an act. I knew I'd make a success of it if I come into this game ... I always had the gift of being able to get on with people and communicate.

The initial relationship between the company and its agent

Having established what types of people were recruited, how were they found? And what was their initial relationship with their employer?

It should be remembered that becoming an agent was not necessarily the first time that there had been a relationship between that person and the company. Some agents or members of their families might have been customers before they became agents and so the business was sometimes quite familiar to them.

Most companies advertised in local newspapers for agents. Companies also paid bonuses, for example £25, for a recommendation from an existing agent. While existing agents were often keen to earn extra money, they had some concerns about recommending people in case they did not turn out to be good agents. A bad recommendation would not make them popular with the management. Sometimes companies took over smaller companies and in such cases, it made sense to keep the existing agents as long as they were performing well.

Managers disliked recruiting new agents. This was not solely due to the time, money and unpredictability involved with any recruitment. It was also due to the fact that a new agent would have to establish relationships with many customers from scratch and business would probably be slow while they were doing this. As one manager explained,

We find that if you get a new agent they won't sell for two, three, four weeks. But once people know that's the regular then they start selling. It's strange, people are like that. When they see a new face at the door, they sort of open and pay you and sort of shut the door quick, because they don't know who you are.

This seems to reflect the element of trust which was at the heart of the relationship between lender and borrower. Customers only started to borrow once they got to know and could judge how far they could trust the lender.

During the observation work, some customers were initially concerned when they saw that their agent was being accompanied. They assumed that the agent was leaving and was showing the ropes to their successor. Many looked relieved when they were told that this was not the case.

Agents received some initial training when they were taken on by a company. Some companies had training manuals and some had even developed computer-based training tools. But most training was on-the-job. Agents were taken on a round by one of the managers or a fellow collector and shown what to do. It was then over to them. As mentioned above, the first few weeks and months of an agent's life could be difficult. One manager explained why,

> *The first three months are really difficult. The first time out on their own they tend to panic because 'I can't find this street' and 'I can't find this house'. And they're handling cash, sometimes for the first time, so they panic ... but I find that if you get them over the first three months you tend to keep them then for some time.*

Some people do leave the business and may look for work elsewhere. Others may leave a particular company but take work with another one. One of the agents interviewed as part of this study had left their previous company because they felt that the company was encouraging people to buy more than they really wanted and get into more debt than was necessary. This agent had stayed in the company for three months but,

> *I was ready to go out of my mind. Every week it was, 'you're going out with this fellah on his van,' and I'm afraid I'm not the type to want to go and sit in a great big van with a fellah, pull up outside somebody's house and expect people to come outside and do it in the street ... it was just a case of 'it doesn't matter what they've got, just put more, more, more in there'. That's how it seemed to me and I couldn't cope with that.*

The agent left that company to work for another. The new company was better than the last, but the agent still felt slightly uneasy at the pressure to increase sales and reach particular targets.

Information from the companies suggests that the average length of experience of their agents varied from an average of four years in one company to fifteen years in another. The agents interviewed in the study had all been agents for at least a couple of years. The full-time male agents had all been in the business much longer than the part-time female agents.

For most agents, there was no career structure in the company and if they stayed in the business they stayed as agents. But in one company, there was evidence that some former agents had become section managers and even branch managers. This was also the only company where women were prominent in managerial posts.

Going into business as a moneylender

So far we have looked at agents of moneylending companies, but there are about 400 sole or small traders where the owner of the company is often the collector as well. There were three routes into this type of business: setting up a company from scratch, buying an existing company and inheriting the family firm.

Two small or sole traders were interviewed during the study. They had gone into business as moneylenders for reasons similar to those of others who became agents: the opportunity to work for oneself and the involvement with people were the main attractions. Both had worked in various jobs before switching to moneylending.

One of the owner-collectors was in his 60s and had had various jobs, mostly self-employed. In the late 1970s, after he was made redundant from a retail credit company he eventually decided to try setting up his own weekly collected credit business. He had a friend with such a business and paid him for some existing customers. Then he worked hard to advertise and build up the rounds. The business had been successful enough for him to have a reasonable standard of living.

The other owner-collector had initially been reluctant to go into his family's moneylending business. He had not been particularly proud of the family tradition. After a public school and university education, he had considered going into the church before becoming a teacher. But education had not given him as much job satisfaction as he had hoped, so, reluctantly, he got involved in his family's business. As he put it,

> *If you're a bit ethically minded and perhaps one is thinking of being ordained, you think, 'gosh, look at these rates of charge, how can it be justified?' so you know, that took time. But it was only because I wasn't in it. If you're in it and you're looking at all these arrears and nils and people in difficulty needing to delay their payments, you can see it.*

He was now in his late 50s. Although his background was very different from that of the majority of his customers, this manifested itself more in a kind of paternalism rather than any overt feelings of superiority. There seemed to be a mutual respect between the owner-collector and his customers. So the difference between them was not as much of a barrier as it was between some of the agents who were only slightly different from their customers in terms of background.

Although money was an important motivator for these two self-employed people, it was not the only motivator. Indeed, one owner-collector's business was not making huge profits,

> *It's very very hard because you lose so much business today and it's hard to put it back on. If I can keep that momentum going all the time then I know at least I can pay my bills and run a reasonable car and that's all I ask out of life really.*

The other estimated that his total earnings were £23,500 before tax. This did not include his company car and pension contributions.

Types of owner-collectors

Although only two owner-collectors were interviewed as part of the research, it is possible to hypothesise as to the types of owner-collectors which might exist. It is likely that there are two main types of owner-collectors. One of these is the same as one of the agent types:

- *entrepreneurs* – these owner-collectors came from a slightly higher social class than their customers or had moved away from their working class roots. Some of them might be judgemental about their customers' poor money management or lack of work ethic. They were fairly detached from their customers although they had a relatively good relationship on the surface.

- paternalists – these owner-collectors came from a higher social class. The social distance between borrower and lender led to a form of detached mutual respect. For the lender, this respect bordered on paternalism and for the borrower, this respect bordered on deference.

The nature of the job

In order to understand the nature of the relationship between moneylenders and their customers, it is important to see the context within which each individual relationship exists.

Terms and conditions of employment

Most agents in the study worked as self-employed on a commission basis, ranging from 7 per cent to 10 per cent commission on money collected. The amount collected during the week these agents took part in the study varied from £2,000 to just over £3,500. Pre-tax earnings varied from £140 for one of the part-time agents to £300 for one of the full-timers.

Few agents were given cars as part of the job even though they were essential. One firm explicitly stated that its 10 per cent commission covered 8 per cent for collection, 1 per cent for petrol and 1 per cent for use of a car. But not all firms were apparently so generous.

Along with the basic commission there were several bonuses which agents could earn. In one company there was a £25 bonus for recommending a new agent and some companies gave a bonus of £5 for each new customer. There were also regular sales drives. One company that sold goods as well as lending cash, had regular summer and winter sales promotions. Agents were given a target based on the number of customers in their round and won a bonus if they achieved their target. There were also extra bonuses for those who did the best in their branch and in the region. Some companies also gave 5 per cent commission on sales of goods.

Although self-employment had its attractions, there were also the drawbacks, such as no company pension. As one agent said,

> My top line is £300 a week which looks good on paper, when you pick up your cheque at the end of the month, say 1100, 1200 quid. But then you've got to take your petrol for the job ... there's your tax and insurance, then your pension and holiday pay ... so consequently I've worked for 25 years and had about five or six weeks off in all that time.

Agents were allowed time off for holidays, but as they were self-employed, this time was not paid for so they limited the time they took off. Those who own their owned companies also found it difficult to take time off. If they were part of a sole enterprise, there was no-one who could step in and cover the round while they were away.

Some agents were paid a small basic salary as well as a small commission on collections. The owner-collectors paid themselves a salary rather than working on commission.

Working week

The structure of a moneylender's working week was similar whether they were agents or owner-collectors. The working week tended to run from Thursday or Friday to the following Tuesday or Wednesday. Friday evenings and Saturdays were often normal working days.

The timing of a moneylender's week, like many aspects of the business, was designed to optimise collection and repayment. Customers in work tended to get paid towards the end of the week. Others on benefits often cashed their giros at the beginning of the week. Evening and weekend work was important in order to catch people when they were at home. Customers who were paid once a month or received their giros once a fortnight were often visited over those periods rather than weekly.

Collectors were generally agreed that the more time spent with a customer, the better. This was because it was thought that developing a close relationship with a customer would lead to more sales and better rates of collection. Collectors spent more time with customers they genuinely liked. They also spent more time with better customers, that is, with customers who borrowed and repaid more than others.

The 'time is money' aspect of the job meant that collectors had to weigh up, consciously or sub-consciously, whether a customer was worth another five minutes.

The collection rounds varied greatly in terms of the amount of time spent with customers. The part-time female agents set a blistering pace. One covered 40 households in three hours and ten minutes, which averaged just over 6 minutes a household. This average included the time it took to get inside the car, put on a seatbelt, drive to the call, take off the seatbelt, pick up the book, get out of the car, lock the door, knock on the customer's door, go into the house, do any paper work, count the money, have a chat, come out of the house, unlock the car and get in the car again! Appendix A gives a much fuller picture of the sometimes hectic life of a moneylender.

Another agent had a much more leisurely round. This was not by choice but because he had lost several customers and was having difficulty finding new ones. He would often drive near to the house that he was calling at and then wait 15 minutes until his usual time for visiting them. He would not knock any earlier even if he thought they might be at home. This was because he considered punctuality essential as good manners. Although there were many pauses in the round, the agent did not mind because, as he put it, each call involved *'decent'* money and so he was reluctant to give up the calls. His other working days were not so quiet.

> *Tomorrow I start at seven and I just won't stop. I'll be clock-watching all the time from one place to another ... but this is just the way of things if I want to fit these people in.*

The timing of the round was generally suited to the customer, but every now and then the regular weekly time was not suitable for them. In such cases, the customer asked the collector to call back another time. Others were just not in when the collector called. The collector then had to make a call-back. Call-backs made life difficult for collectors, especially if their round was widely spread out or there was very little spare time between calls.

Timing was essential for many calls. People on a low income may well find something else to spend their money on if the collector does not arrive on the dot.

Geography

Rounds varied greatly in terms of their geographical clustering. One round was virtually restricted to a single council estate, although the estate was said to be one of the biggest in Europe. Other rounds tended to have two or three centres, usually council estates, which the collector travelled within and around. Some rounds were very unclustered and covered a great deal of ground. It was not uncommon for collectors to cover more than 50 miles on a single day.

Even where the usual round looked clustered on paper, this was not necessarily ideal for the collector. Sometimes collectors had several calls in the same road or even next door to each other, but Ms X at Number 6 wanted to be visited on Friday at 6pm, Ms Y at Number 11 wanted to be visited on Saturday at 11.30am and Mr Z at Number 2 wanted to be visited on Monday at 3.30pm.

Agents covered a wide variety of housing types. Few calls were made to high-rise flats but there were many calls to low-rise flats and houses in council estates. In the North, many calls were made to pre-war terraced houses. There were some calls to owner-occupied houses and a few to people in residential homes.

There were some 'no-go' areas. Some agents were reluctant to make calls on some estates and this was often based on actual experience of violence in the area rather than just fear of potential violence. Other agents would sometimes be put onto those estates. But some parts of estates were excluded. These were mainly the high-rise tower blocks. The periphery of two estates (on different rounds) were considered safe, but the agents said that they would not venture into the cores. Both estates were notorious for the sale of drugs and weapons. Some parts of other estates which had to be reached via badly lit paths were also considered too much trouble. This means that people living in these areas would not have access to licensed moneylenders.

Vulnerability

If people consider vulnerability in relation to moneylending, it is usually the customer that springs to mind first of all. The general image of a moneylender is someone who exploits vulnerable people. But there are many ways in which the collector can also be vulnerable.

It is in the nature of the job that collectors were carrying large sums of money with them and were walking in the same streets at the same time every week. They were often an easy target for theft. Some companies devised procedures to improve their agents' safety. These included regular banking and the use of cash received to make further advances. Agents themselves took various precautions to avoid becoming a victim. Collectors were careful about where they put the money that they were given. They also tried to avoid the money being visible in the street. This was not always easy when some customers preferred to deal with the agent on the doorstep.

Several agents tried to avoid working in the dark, but this was difficult during winter evenings. One agent blamed himself for being attacked because he had been visiting a particular estate after dark,

> There's an infamous estate ... and it was after dark and I should not really have been there. I was going to see someone who was not paying too well ... as it was a tower block I caught the lift and I was the only

> *one there at that time. As soon as I got into the lift suddenly there was three big West Indian chaps in the lift with me. They got no money because I did have the intelligence not to take any in there with me. Mind you it didn't do me any good because if they can't find the money they give you a bigger belting ... I ended up with a busted rib.*

The agent was 70 when he was attacked. Now, five years later, he only worked some parts of that estate during daylight hours. No new customers were canvassed from within the estate.

Two of the women agents had had their bags stolen. One had been threatened in the street by a man with his face covered and she gave him her bag. She was very shaken by the experience and did not work for a short time. When she resumed work, she only did so because her husband drove her round to all her calls and waited while she went inside. Another agent had the frightening experience of getting into her car to drive off only to find that someone had got into the back of the car and was demanding her money.

Those collectors who had not experienced attacks generally knew of close colleagues who had.

In one of the small companies, the owner-collector had not been attacked, but the only other collector in the company had been. He had fought back against his attacker and escaped with his money intact. But he had been shaken by the experience.

One agent had a friend who worked for a rival company. This friend had been warned by his customers that some people were out to get his money and that if he were to visit a particular street he would be attacked. The collector was sufficiently scared but knew that he had to do his rounds. He asked another friend to accompany him for safety and he was unharmed. The agent who told this story worked down the same street but he knew from his customers that several people from that street had recently been sent to prison and that their removal would make the street safer, at least for a while.

Collectors were not only vulnerable to attack from people. The areas they worked in were also inhabited by potentially dangerous dogs. The agent who had been attacked in the lift had also been the victim of a dog. He thought it quite ironic that the owners had a perfect record with their repayments,

> *They were 'one-hundred-per-cent-ers' to me but this guard dog! They invited me into the hall and the dog just had a great big lump out of my thigh, ripped all my trousers down which they thought was a huge joke!*

Most of the collectors knew all the dogs of their customers and so were not quite so scared of them. But sometimes when collectors knocked on the door there would be fierce barking, followed by a customer saying that they were just putting the dog into another room. The front door was then opened but the barking could still be heard in the background and there was often a slight doubt about what might happen if a dog got loose or if a customer got angry and the dog sensed this. One agent told of a time when one of his customers came up to put her arms around him. He was not very keen on the customer and so tried to push her away playfully, but the dog did not like this and tore a hole in his trousers.

Some of the company managers played down the personal risks to their agents saying that they were not high. The reactions of the collectors themselves varied. Some were frightened, especially if they had experienced an attack. Others knew the areas they were working in very well and so felt less threatened and felt that if they stayed in the appropriate areas at appropriate times, they would not have to worry about their safety.

KEY POINTS

- There are about 1200 licensed moneylending companies in the UK.

- The credit provided by these companies is very expensive with APRs varying from 100 to 500 per cent.

- There are about 27,000 people who lend and collect money from door-to-door.

- Most collectors are women working as agents for the larger companies. Some collectors work for themselves or employ one or two other collectors apart from themselves.

- Companies are looking for agents who get on well with customers but who can also detach themselves from customers and maintain loyalty to the interests of the company.

- People become agents because they are attracted to the hours of work, the pay, the opportunities for self-employment and the interaction with people.

- Collectors are vulnerable to being attacked in the street by people who know that they are carrying large sums of money with them. Three of the eight collectors in the study had been the victims of such an attack.

---

3   The Customers

Our best estimate is that there are about 3 million customers of licensed moneylenders in the UK. The stereotypical image of a moneylender's customer is someone who is very poor and desperate for money due to their dire financial situation. The companies that took part in this study were asked about the demographic profile of their customers. One of the large companies had access to information from a large-scale customer survey but the smaller companies only had their best guesses to go on. From this information, it seems that the majority of customers of moneylending companies are between the ages of 30 and 60. The majority are in work, but a sizeable minority are either unemployed, 'economically inactive' or retired. A small majority are women, but couples may tend to put a loan in the husband's name even though the loan will be for joint purposes and the woman will deal with the collector. So it is probable that most of the people who actually deal with the moneylender on the doorstep will be women. These findings certainly correspond to the information collected on the observation rounds of this study.

The type of customer that companies and agents are looking for
Companies were looking to recruit customers who would borrow large sums of money and pay for it all according to the original terms of the credit agreement. Such customers would be both able and willing to pay back large loans. The worst customers were seen as those who borrowed a great deal of money and then did not pay it back. Managers and agents were well aware of the view that they take on customers who cannot afford to borrow from them. They defended themselves by saying that it was not good practice, from a purely economic point of view, to recruit such customers.

This section looks at the types of people whom the companies and agents thought would be both willing and able to repay large loans.

Social and economic characteristics

Workers were usually preferred to non-workers as customers. At one time, one company had not taken on any unemployed customers in the South of England. But with the recession in the South they realised that there were a large number of potential customers who had very little alternative source of credit.

Workers were seen as potentially good customers because of their relatively large disposable income. But there was always the risk of lending according to ability rather than willingness to repay. There was often a doubt in the back of a moneylender's mind that if someone said that they were in a very stable, well-paid job, why don't they go to an alternative and cheaper source of credit? Such customers might well have been credit referenced to see if they have a tendency to borrow but not a corresponding tendency to pay back. But generally, workers were considered more respectable and trustworthy than unemployed people.

One difficulty, however, with someone in paid work, was that there was no way of knowing how secure someone's job might be. If a worker was lent a large sum and then lost their job, they would not be able to pay back according to the terms of the original agreement. Unemployed people generally had less disposable income but at least it was regular and reliable. They would probably be very grateful for the money as they would have little access to other sources and so they might be very careful to keep up repayments. Also, for most unemployed people, the only way was up. If an unemployed person managed to repay a small loan according to terms the chances were that if and when they found work they would be an even better customer.

Some managers were concerned about taking on some of the very poorest people. Some of their current customers might have become very poor due to circumstances which the agent could not foresee, but those who were very poor would not be taken on as new customers.

Age was seen by collectors as another important characteristic which guided decision-making. Younger people in work who were still living at home might well have had a reasonably high disposable income. But they were not considered to be as responsible and trustworthy as older people. As one agent explained,

> *All these youngsters don't have the same outlook on life as their parents, you know. The older people pay like good-uns but the*

youngsters want everything but they don't want to pay anything – that can be the biggest problem ... sometimes you get a spin-off from the parents, you know, kids you've known all their lives and that's OK.

The agent also thought that younger people were more likely to get access to other sources of credit and so were less likely to come to his firm.

Young people were generally taken on as customers when their parents were existing customers and the moneylender had known them for some time. This gave the collectors an opportunity to assess their trustworthiness. It also meant that if 'mum' had a good relationship with the moneylender then she might keep an eye on her child and make sure they repaid their loan.

People in their 50s and above were considered the most responsible and trustworthy but those aged over 60 were risky because they might die just after borrowing a large sum of money. After a certain age, companies could not insure for death and so the money was often lost. The deceased customer might have left some money to clear the debt, but this was unusual. Sometimes their family wanted to clear the debt so that their relative could not be said to have died a debtor. But the debt was not always cleared and so most companies were reluctant to take on new customers who were over 60 and many agents were actively trying to reduce the amount lent to existing customers over that age.

Certain family types had question marks against them. Lone parents were one such group according to some companies and agents. This was partly because of their financial circumstances but also because they were considered less respectable and trustworthy. During one of the observation rounds, one of the owner-collectors received a telephone call from a lone parent who wanted a loan. He did not immediately assume that she would be a bad payer but said that the risk of it was too high,

I'm not willing to take the chance, not now. I don't want to know that sort of business. When you first start, you tend to take a few more gambles.

People living in particular housing estates or blocks of flats were also unlikely to be given credit by moneylenders. This was not because of the type of people but because of the dangers involved in working those areas. The core area of certain estates was often considered too dangerous. As mentioned earlier, one agent had been attacked in one of these areas. Another agent was taking preventive action with a similar estate,

> *In the [estate] you've got the multi big buildings in the middle, in the shopping area which is, well, I wouldn't touch it with a barge pole. I used to when I started but there's been muggings there. Plenty of women collectors have been mugged and it's notorious. But the perimeter is much different. You've still got to be careful, there was a murder there a few weeks ago at night in the perimeter, right beside where I call actually. But generally that's not bad and this is my best call in [the estate]. What does [Jack] pay me? £90 a week.*

In this case, the collector was willing to take what he considered a slight risk to collect almost £100.

The same collector also knew about the estate where the other collector had been attacked,

> *Well that ... estate. When I first started I had a couple of customers on the safer side ... but on the left side even the police wouldn't go at one time. It was absolutely uncontrollable with drugs and yardies and all that. On the other side it was bad but not that bad and I was very innocent when I first went into that area.*

He no longer went onto that estate.

There were also problems in gaining access to flats now that entryphone systems were more widespread. As one manager said, this made it easier for customers to avoid their collector,

> *Our basic customer is the normal council-house tenant and the ones that we avoid are flat-dwellers because they can hide ... and some of them you can't even get access to now because you press the button downstairs and they've got to let you in – those sort of flats we don't want to know.*

Another manager mentioned similar difficulties,

> *The only time we go into a high rise flat is if someone [an existing customer] actually moved in. We don't canvas high rise flats at all ... there are security doors on now so you can't get into them and with a flat you can't look in the garden and through the kitchen window.*

By high-rise flats, many managers meant any with more than two storeys, not just tower blocks.

So the ideal customer was thought to be an honest, middle-aged worker in a stable family. People who were officially unemployed were slightly more desirable as customers than lone parents or pensioners. The least attractive customers were people who were desperate for money or living in particular areas.

Some individuals who had been particularly bad customers in the past were unlikely to be taken back as customers after a break. These people were often put on a 'Don't Serve' (DS) list. One manager explained,

> *We actually keep a DS list and [an agent] was out a couple of weeks ago ... and there was someone who was very very rude to her, you know, threatened to set the dog on her. So she went back to the section manager and said, 'I'm never knocking on that door again'. So that door has gone on the DS list.*

Sometimes these people slipped through the net because DS lists were often kept in managers' and agents' heads. Where they did exist on paper they were not always checked thoroughly.

Some collectors were concerned that rival companies might take on these people as customers. They tried to warn their competitors about these people by marking doors or doorposts. One collector explained that he looked out for,

> *... a scratch down the side where somebody's used a sharp tool ... NBG that's the usual one – No Bloody Good!*

One collector was careful to check the customer's door for any possible tell-tale signs,

> *The first thing I look for is pin-holes, where they've left everybody else that's selling to call next week! ... Another sign to sort of delve into is if you arrive during the course of the day, say midday, the front room curtains are drawn ... that's worth another visit ... that's another commonplace sign, you know, that people are running up debt somewhere and don't want to see anybody.*

Although moneylenders often assumed that particular social or economic characteristics would be linked to particular personality traits, they also attempted to identify these traits directly.

Personality traits

It was relatively easy to check whether a prospective customer had the ability to repay a loan. For example, wage slips were checked if they were in work. But it was much more difficult to know whether they had the willingness to repay a loan because this depended on their personality. Agents had to judge how far they thought they could trust a customer.

Most managers and agents agreed that you couldn't necessarily judge respectability, trustworthiness and honesty by appearance. As one of the owner-collectors said of the people who visited the company office,

> *People come in here very smart and you think, 'they're fine' and it doesn't work like that I'm afraid. You can get the opposite and they're marvellous!*

One of the managers was very proud of her detective-like skills. She used every piece of information when assessing whether to take someone on as a new customer,

> *You look, you look and you listen ... say a young couple and there's not a lot in the house and they say they've got no credit, that I could believe. If they've got loads in the house, someone's telling you porkies ... if it's like today [very cold] and you go into someone's house and there's no heating on you think, 'oh! Can they afford the heating?'*

In these cases, the manager was looking for honesty in the potential customer as well as ability to repay.

Many managers and collectors said that they used their 'instinct' when deciding whether to take someone on as a new customer. As one of them said,

> *I've been dealing with the public one way or another most of my life you know and it's like a policeman, he gets these gut feelings and my gut feelings and reactions are pretty good. And I think 90% of the times I'm right.*

But the company's ideal customer was not exactly the same as the collector's. Of course the collector wanted someone who borrowed and repaid well. But they were also keen to have a customer that they liked. One of the female agents suffered sexual harassment from the friend of a customer, but was reluctant to give the customer up. Instead she took as much avoiding action as she could, which included having her husband with her when she called at that house. Other dislikes were not so serious. But collectors often talked about some customers who bored or irritated them. On the other hand, there were some customers who did not borrow much or who were slow at repaying but whom they liked very much on a personal level. So while the company was solely concerned with the business aspects of the relationship, the collector had other considerations.

Taking on new customers
New customers were recruited through personal recommendation, canvassing and advertising. Once a potential new customer was found, the application process was fairly informal.

Methods of recruiting customers
Most managers and collectors agreed that the best way of recruiting good customers was through personal recommendation. As one manager said,

> We try to be very careful who we take on. We tend to only take on relatives of people on the books or friends. But if friends recommend it, the person recommending has to guarantee it to start off with.

Personal recommendation was seen as the safest way of recruiting customers because a collector would know whether they could trust the opinion of the existing customer. And if the existing customer guaranteed the first loan then the collector could be even more sure that the money would be repaid.

One collector had a recommendation from an existing customer who then warned him that her friend only paid well at first,

> [Carol] introduced her to me and I can't complain about her, you know, she's pays me very very well. It must be about 18 months, two years now. I've got the daughter on the books and the daughter pays me alright. But of course now she's forewarned me, now I've got to be careful in the future ... [Carol] thinks that she drops off after a while you see.

But recommendations were, of themselves, insufficient to generate all the new customers that the businesses wanted and most of the medium and large companies also employed canvassers to expand their customer base for their agents. Canvassing cash loans is illegal, so companies canvassed goods instead. This could be anything from a Christmas food hamper, to a first-aid kit, to a duvet cover. Once someone decided to buy goods they were visited by a collector the following week and are eventually informed of the availability of cash loans.

One of the large companies had very sophisticated geo-demographic marketing tools. It was able to highlight which areas were most likely to provide good customers, for example areas with a high concentration of lower-middle and working-class people of working age. It could then look at which of these areas had a lower than average proportion of existing customers. Such areas were then targeted by canvassers. Other companies, without such resources, would use local knowledge to judge which areas would be best to canvas. Of course it was always useful to canvas in neighbourhoods were there already were existing customers so that the time taken to make a call was as short as possible.

Managers, specialist canvassers and sometimes agents themselves would visit the selected areas and take examples of goods with them to encourage custom. Sometimes a van or lorry would tour the area full of items. People who bought goods in these circumstances were usually only allowed a small amount of credit, such as £50. When collecting the repayments, the agent then had time to judge whether the customer would be able and willing to repay a further loan.

Agents were often initially sceptical about customers who had been recruited by canvassers. Canvassers were usually paid according to how many people they managed to sell things to rather than how many people were likely to pay back the amount lent. One agent was particularly scathing of canvassers because they sometimes served ex-customers of hers that she did not want to deal with again. Agents often complained that canvassed calls were 'trouble' because too many people had no intention of repaying and yet they, the agents, still had to visit them every week. Even where the new customer did pay, this was often a small amount of money, maybe £2 or £3 a week. This might lead to bigger and better things, but not always.

One agent said that he did his best to get rid of bad customers, but then after a canvasser had done his work there were always more to 'weed out'.

> I haven't got much rubbish though because you weed the rubbish out
> ... Where I've finished up with a bit of rubbish is when they have to
> send out the canvassers and they canvas an area and I could go in
> there Monday morning, you could say there's 15 calls in [one area],
> then you don't know what they're like and you finish up, you might
> get three out of that 15 that are really good, the rest are, some are

mediocre and others are a real dead loss that you can't get the money out of at all.

One agent said that he had recently picked up five new customers on one estate through canvassers. One had literally disappeared after the first week. One was very difficult to find at home. Two were reasonable payers but were unlikely to want any more business. Only one was likely to remain a medium- or long-term customer and would probably buy some more goods when her initial loan finished.

So canvassers were seen as something of a mixed blessing by collectors. They may have been good at selling and therefore recruiting potential new customers. But, unlike the agents who would take the customers over from them, they were not concerned about either the ability or willingness to pay.

Most of the smaller companies could not afford to employ specialist canvassers. Instead, they advertised their services, for example, in a local newsagent. But one of the owner-collectors was concerned about the risks involved with taking new customers from such sources,

> *I don't get a lot of recommendations on my particular round ... the way I do it is only round advertising shop boards. I find that you do tend to get a lot of the bad element that phone you up because you're a new company or it's the first time they've seen you or they've moved into the area and they think, 'ah, we'll try that company, try and take them on.' So you have to be selective and very very careful, you know. You get a small percentage out of it that are good accounts.*

When a potential customer is found, managers and agents will find out what they can about them through talking to them and looking at their homes. They will find out about their financial means and try to judge willingness to repay the loan by using their 'instinct'. The key thing, mentioned by all agents and managers, was to start new customers off slowly. If they repay a £50 loan well, they will then be able to borrow a bit more, then a bit more. During this time, the agent will get to know the customer and will look for signs that the customer will continue to be a good payer. But there were pressures on managers and agents to give larger loans at first. As one manager explained,

> *We don't really give people more than £50 or £100 to start with. Now maybe that's right or wrong, I don't know. But all our loans are unsecured, we only have to go on face value until we get to know people. And a lot of our customers have been with us 20 years,*

> *sometimes more, but it takes a long time to get to know someone, so that's why we keep it to a low amount. A lot of people don't like it and they say, 'no, I need £500, thanks very much, cheerio!' Maybe we're losing business, I don't know ... we do do £500 loans but not until we really know people and we need to know that they can afford to pay.*

At the back of many collectors' minds was the fear that a new customer might be, as one collector put it, a *'borrower shark'*. An example given by one collector was a new customer who borrows £50 and repays that initial loan without any problem. They then build up the collector's trust, borrowing ever increasing amounts until they get a big loan and then refuse to pay anything or move home without a trace. Of course, if that default is for 'genuine' reasons, the customer would not be blamed. But the fear was that some people were deliberately building up the collector's trust in order to defraud them. All collectors had this fear of, what they variously called, *'borrower sharks'*, *'knockers'* and *'professional debtors'* or simply *'professionals'*. Creditors in all fields have similar fears of a group they label collectively as the 'won't pays' who deliberately 'work the system'.

One way of checking people out is to run a credit reference check on them. Credit referencing systems are operated by specialist agencies and are usually accessed by an on-line computer network or by telephone. A reference usually involves three checks. First, the borrower's name and address are verified against the appropriate electoral register. Then a search is made for county court judgements recorded against the borrower in the past six years. Finally, information is checked about arrears with any of the other subscribers to the system. Until now, it has only been possible to record 'black' information, that is, information about arrears. But lenders are also keen to know about whether prospective customers have been particularly good payers through access to 'white' information.

But collectors did not always do this. This is partly because of the cost and effort involved but also because of the difficulties in interpreting the reference. Not all creditors pursue bad debtors to the point of having a County Court Judgement taken out against them. So the absence of CCJs on a credit reference is no guarantee that the person will be a good customer. Nor can the presence of a CCJ prove that a customer will be a bad payer in the future. One manager said that he would ask a prospective customer if they had any CCJs. If the person said they did, this was actually counted as a positive sign of honesty. If they said they did not and then were subsequently found to have them, this was taken as a very bad sign – not only had they been a bad payer in the past, they were also currently dishonest. In this case at least, credit references were used in subtle ways to check personality traits.

Surprisingly, perhaps, there was some evidence that companies cooperated in vetting potential customers. We mentioned earlier how collectors sometimes warned others about bad customers by inscribing DS (Don't Serve) or NBG (No Bloody Good) into their doorposts. There was also some evidence of local credit referencing. One collector said that in the past there had been a local cafe that many collectors frequented to swap stories about their customers. One manager admitted that even today,

> *We are in touch with other traders, we have to be. And if there's any doubt we'll ring up and say, 'do you know anything about this person?' Because we try to help each other in the trade obviously ... we tend to credit reference locally rather than nationally because the local situation's known by the trade and we don't take anybody out of the blue, can't afford to do it.*

But there was also, of course, competition for customers. Collectors were concerned about taking on people who might be bad customers, but they were also concerned that they might lose a potentially good customer to another company. And there were other parts of the credit industry who might pick off the very best customers.

So there was a mixture of competition and cooperation within the industry. As one manager explained,

> *You go to a customer's house and I bet you any money most of them have got two or three people calling round a week, most of them have, if they've got one they've got two or three and that's how they live. And it may be that at times when it gets to be a bit tight, they'll pay one one week and pay another another week. But it's not us preying on them, it's just because that's the way they tend to live and they see somebody else come along initially with a pair of sheets or something like that, 'oh I like those, yes' and they go into that. And we've got a lot of competition but a lot of us have got together to protect ourselves, not as a cartel type thing but just ourselves in the CCA. And we tend to sort of, without going into individual customers, we get together and talk about the way things are and how things are going.*

The application process

Becoming a customer of a moneylender is a much less formal process than it is for other consumer credit. For most types of credit, people become customers by filling in an application form giving details about their current situation. This form-filling usually takes place in a bank, building society or shop. Sometimes the form can be filled in at home and sent to the prospective lender. The details from the form are then assessed in a process known as application scoring. This is a statistical technique which assesses the probability of a given type of borrower repaying an advance. Credit scorecards are built on an analysis of the characteristics and payment records of previous borrowers. Characteristics which are associated with a high probability of timely repayments are given high scores, those with low probabilities are given low scores. The total score is added up and if the applicant has reached the 'pass mark' their application will be accepted. The pass mark will be set by the lender and will reflect the amount of risk they are prepared to take.

Application scoring only takes into account the economic and social characteristics of applicants. The most common characteristics relate to economic activity, age, current use of credit and housing tenure. No measurement is made of more personal characteristics. Someone who is young, living in a council house and unemployed or working in a low-paid job would probably not reach the 'pass mark' of many lenders.

In contrast, moneylenders use a much less formal system although they do, on occasion, check credit references and at the outset of a relationship an application form is likely to be used. Moneylenders take into account personal as well as social and economic characteristics of prospective customers. These personal characteristics include honesty, trustworthiness and reliability. Moneylenders argue that this means they do not discriminate against particular groups of people, such as the unemployed or council tenants, as the banks may discriminate. They judge each applicant individually.

For example, the young, low-paid council tenant who will find it difficult to get a bank loan might be able to get credit from a moneylender. This will depend on what the moneylender knows about their circumstances and their personality. Perhaps the young, low-paid council tenant's mother has been a customer for many years. She has always been a good payer and is a very 'respectable' woman. The moneylender has seen the young person grow up and knows them quite well. In such a case, the prospective customer may well be lent money. But if the young person is not known to the collector or they show signs of being untrustworthy they may not be successful in being given a loan.

The types of people who become customers

We have seen that moneylenders try to attract working couples to be customers. And indeed, the majority of customers interviewed were in exactly this situation when they first borrowed from a moneylender. It is important to remember, however, that the people interviewed are not representative of all new customers. They are all people who have stayed on as customers. It may be that some groups of people become customers and then discontinue with the moneylender. These groups will not be represented here.

Table 4 gives some details about their situations when they first became customers.

The child-rearing years are the peak time for using credit of all types (Berthoud and Kempson 1992) and the customers of moneylenders were no exception to this. More than half (17) of the 31 people interviewed had been in couples with young children when they first became customers. This was a period when money was getting tighter as there were more mouths to feed and less income to go round. All of these families had some form of paid work at the time they became customers. In most of the couples the man was in full-time manual employment; only a few of the wives were also in employment, and then only part-time. There was also one example of a couple where the only employment was very casual and so the family were living on a combination of benefits and wages.

One couple had migrated Southwards just before the Second World War. He found work in the steel industry and she worked in the home looking after their children. They became customers of a moneylender in the 1950s to pay for bills and buy clothes for their children. In more recent times, a young couple had both had paid jobs when they first got together. She had worked in a bank and he had been a security guard. After the birth of their second child the woman gave up her job. Her partner's work became more insecure and eventually she took some work as a child-minder. It was during this time that she became a customer.

Table 4   Characteristics of customers at the time they first borrowed

Family type	Age	Year	What moneylender was used for
Young single woman	21	1947	Clothes
	24	1952	Clothes
	23	1973	Household goods
	20	1975	Clothes
	17	1978	Clothes
	22	1983	Holiday spending money
	18	1988	Jewellery, clothes
	24	1990	Jewellery
Couple with children	33	1953	Bills and clothes for children
	24	1954	Clothes etc for children
	35	1960	Clothes etc for children
	25	1963	Clothes etc for children
	33	1963	Clothes etc for children
	25	1965	Clothes etc for children
	35	1965	Clothes etc for children
	23	1983	Blanket
	35	1983	Bills
	32	1986	Bills
	30	1988*	Hamper
	32	1988*	Household goods
	32	1988*	First-aid box
	35	1988*	Living expenses
	38	1988*	First-aid box
	23	1989	Rented TV
	24	1993	Duvet set
Lone parent	25	1989	Decorating
Older couple	60	1980	Wedding anniversary
	55	1982	Bills
Older single	60	1981	Bills
	34	1983	Clothes
	55	1986	Bills

*   Some people found it difficult to say exactly when they became customers and guessed that it was about 5 years ago – hence the apparent concentration of new customers in 1988.

The next largest group of new customers were younger than the couples. About a quarter (8) of the 31 people interviewed had been young, single women when they had first become customers. These women had been brought up in families who had used moneylending, and usually the same collector, in the past. A few years after getting a job, it seemed the appropriate thing to join in the family tradition and take out a loan to buy clothes or jewellery. Usually these people were still living at home paying little rent. They had been in low-paid work for a year or two after leaving school and so they had the means to repay a loan. And they were keen for the opportunity to acquire various consumer goods.

One woman had first borrowed from the collector just after her 18th birthday to buy clothes. Her parents had used the collector for many years and both her sisters now used the same company. Some of the longest-serving customers had also first used the company when they were single and living with their families. One customer first used the company in 1947. Like her parents, she bought clothes on credit from the company shop. Another customer had first bought goods from the company in 1951. She recalled that she was following in her grandmother's footsteps.

Although most people became customers either when they were young and single or when they were living as a couple and had young children, there were six customers who did not come into either of these categories. One was a lone parent who borrowed some money to decorate her house. One was a woman in her 50s who had a partner. They were finding it difficult to manage on their low income and borrowed to help with bills and general expenses. Three were single people moving into middle age or old age before first turning to a moneylender. One of these was a woman in her late 50s. She had recently been divorced from her husband and was finding it difficult to manage without income from him. Another started using the company when he found it difficult to manage after leaving his job due to ill health.

It is sometimes thought that people become customers of a moneylender because they are in a dire financial situation and have no alternative source of funds. When they first borrowed from a moneylender the couples were generally borrowing to provide basics such as children's shoes and clothes. Sometimes they had borrowed to pay bills or buy bedding and other essential furniture. But in virtually all cases, the man in the couple was working at the time of first borrowing and so there was a weekly wage from which the loan could be repaid. And in some cases, these people were only buying very small items with small weekly repayments. One couple had bought a first aid box from a canvasser. Another woman only had £2.50 a week to repay and her partner was in work so this was not difficult to find.

The young women were certainly not desperate for money or goods at the time they became customers. They were keen to acquire certain goods and had the money to repay the amount borrowed.

The other people – lone parents and older people without children – were most likely to have started using the company when they were in difficult financial situations. One woman in her late 50s had got into debt with various creditors after her husband left her. She was living on a much reduced income and had not been used to managing money. Fortunately, she had two daughters who were able to help her out, but she increasingly disliked her dependence on her daughters. She was desperate to gain some financial independence and so contacted a moneylender.

All of this describes the people as they were when they first became customers and, for the most part, they reflected what the companies were looking for. But some people remained as customers for many years and so were in very different situations when they were interviewed. So the current stock of customers may not reflect what the companies want.

Figure 1 shows the situations of customers when they first used a moneylender and when they were interviewed. It shows that nine of the 31 customers were in couples with dependent children at the time of the interview. Five were couples of working age with adult children. Four were lone parents. Three were single people of working age who were sick or disabled. And ten were over pension age – four single people and six couples.

All the lone parents were women as were all four of the single pensioners. Two of the three older single people were men. In most of the couples, the woman gave the interview as she had most, if not sole, dealings with the moneylender. But in some cases, both members of the couple participated in the interview just as they both participated in dealing with the moneylender.

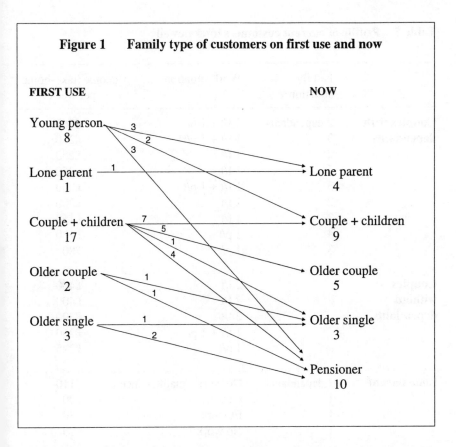

Figure 1   Family type of customers on first use and now

Only three of the nine couples with dependants were dual earner families (see table 5). In a further four couples, the man alone was in (full-time but often casual) work. The other two couples were without a full-time earner at the time they were interviewed. In one case the man was unemployed and was looking for work as a carpenter although at the time of the interview, he was away on holiday with some friends. His partner worked 14 hours a week and earned £40. On top of this she received £90 Income Support a fortnight for herself, her partner and their three young children. They should probably have been receiving more than this, but her work situation changed quite rapidly. In the other couple, he was a labourer whose work was sporadic and often at very short notice. His family lived on a combination of work and benefits. He did not always declare his earnings to the DSS when he was legally obliged to do so.

Table 5   Profile of current customers interviewed

	Family situation	Work situation	Income (take-home per week
Couples with dependants	2 dependants	1 f/t + 1 p/t	£360
	3	1 f/t + 1 p/t	£270
	2	1 f/t	£250
	5	1 f/t	£250
	3	1 f/t + 1 p/t	£230
	2	1 f/t	£200
	2	1 f/t	£150
	4	1 p/t	£150
	3	1 p/t	£80
Couples without dependants		2 f/t	£400
		2 f/t	£400
		2 f/t	£300
		1 f/t + 1 p/t	£250
		1 p/t	£225
Lone parent	2 dependants	No work - maintenance	£110
	1	p/t work	£90
	1	f/t work	£80
	1	No work	£70
Older single		Disabled	£60
		Disabled	£70
		Disabled	£90
Pensioners	Couple	No work - occup. pension	£200
	Couple	p/t work	£160
	Couple	No work - occup. pension	£140
	Couple	p/t work	£130
	Couple	Disabled	£125
	Couple	Disabled	£120
	Single	Disabled + maintenance	£120
	Single	p/t work	£80
	Single	No work	£70
	Single	No work	£60

Four of the five older couples without dependent children were dual earner families. One couple was probably better off than any other family in the study. They were in their 40s. She was a secretary bringing home about £250 a week. He was a manual worker earning about £150. Their children were no longer at school, but still lived at home.

One of the four lone parents was living solely on income support. Another received maintenance on top of her income support. Another received earnings from a few hours of work and one worked 25 hours a week. This last lone parent was missing out on a very large amount of family credit which she could have claimed if she had known about it. She had a one year-old child and was earning £77 a week. She could have claimed about £48 in family credit.

All the workers did similar jobs. The men were nearly all full-time manual workers. For example, they delivered milk, did maintenance work in factories, were drivers, security guards and cleaners. Most of the women who had paid jobs were working part-time, for example as cleaners and shop assistants. Most of them were receiving too much in wages to be eligible for family credit but one couple was entitled to about £7 a week. They were not aware of this and were not claiming the benefit.

One of the disabled customers had become a customer when he left the army and needed some money to ease his transition back to civvy street. He had then found work only to suffer an accident which disabled him. One of the other disabled customers was rather vague about her disability. At one point she said that she *'gave up work'* to help out her daughter when she became a teenage lone parent. But since that time she had received invalidity benefit. She had become a customer at about the same time.

Four of the ten pensioners were single. The remaining six were living with a partner. Before they had retired, most of the men had been skilled, manual workers, in similar jobs to the younger male customers. Fewer of the women had worked. All of the pensioners had become customers before they reached retirement. Three had been customers for more than 40 years. Only two of these pensioners, both single women, were living solely on income support. Three had income from disability benefits, such as disability living allowance and invalid care allowance. One of these also received sporadic maintenance from the husband she had recently separated from. Two couples had occupational pensions which actually raised them slightly above income support levels. And a further three couples and one single pensioner supplemented their basic pensions with earnings from part-time jobs.

This gives us a picture of the current circumstances of customers in the sample, although it is important to stress again that this demographic mix may not be totally representative of the current customer base of the industry as a whole. Most of the couples of working age had at least one earner in the family. The lone parents and pensioners did little paid work between them. But although we might assume that the workers were better off than the non-workers, many of them had very large numbers of children. One couple had five children aged 7, 5, 3, 2 and a two month old baby. The man's earnings from delivering milk were just enough to pay for the basic necessities of life. Another couple had six children aged 20, 18, 17, 16, 14 and 7 years old respectively. Although not all of these were still dependent on their parents, there had been a time when there were many mouths to feed and backs to clothe. Another couple in their 30s had four children aged 7, 5, 4 and 1 year old. So even the workers, who were primarily in manual jobs, found that their wages did not go very far. It was only the five couples with no dependants who had incomes about or above average.

Ways of using a moneylender

Critics argue that people are desperate for money when they borrow from a moneylender and they use this form of credit to buy basic necessities and pay bills. The industry claims that customers are using a moneylender to obtain consumer durables and improve their quality of life. The research found that there were three main ways in which people used their moneylender.

About a third (11) of the customers interviewed used credit from a moneylender to help provide consumer goods. Some of these bought very small items for their families or home. Others took out large loans for 'luxury' items such as CD players, camcorders and foreign holidays.

One of the lone parents had borrowed £700 in July for a camcorder. She was paying the company a total of about £1100 for the £700 principal amount at £21 a week for 52 weeks (an APR of 168 per cent). If she had been able to put away £21 a week herself, it would only have taken about 33 weeks to save for the camcorder (not counting interest paid to her) rather than paying the same amount over 52 weeks. Or, to put it another way, she would only have had to save £13.50 a week over 52 weeks. But she knew that, with a young daughter to look after, she would not have been able to save. Although she was paying heavily for it, the company was enabling her to finance a luxury item which she could not have bought any other way.

One woman on a low income also used the company to save for a luxury which she would otherwise have not been able to afford. This was her annual holiday abroad. She was now in her 60s and had used the company off and on for 40 years. Her grandmother had also used the company. She had first become a customer when she was single and continued to use the company when she had children. Now she borrowed £700 every year to pay for her holiday. She had been going to the same resort now for many years since the agent first suggested borrowing the money for a holiday. She had built up several relationships at the holiday resort and her holiday was now the highlight of her year. But she was now 64 and there was a threat that she would be forcibly retired from her cleaning job. Without the earnings of £40 a week which supplemented her pension, she would not be able to afford her £21 a week repayments.

A further third (9) customers used credit from a moneylender as a way of smoothing over the ups and downs caused by their changing income levels. For these people, who had had insecure jobs and periods in and out of employment, money from a moneylender was seen as the one stable source of "income" during their lives. They knew that they could rely on a certain amount of money coming in every few months. When times were good, for example, when there was overtime or some extra part-time work, credit was used to buy consumer goods. When times were bad, credit was used to help pay for bills and essentials.

The remaining third (11) customers used credit from a moneylender almost exclusively as a way of managing their meagre resources. They were living long-term on low income and found it difficult to save up for bills and provide any basic household goods. Most of these people were pensioners.

People could move from one type of use to another as their circumstances changed. Generally, young, single people started to use a moneylender solely to buy consumer goods but once they had a family they switched to using credit to smooth over the ups and downs. Then when the children grew up they returned to consumerism before using it for help with the bills after retirement.

Table 6 shows the relationship between current family type and the way people used a moneylender.

Table 6   Relationship between current family type and way of using a moneylender

	Couples with children	Lone parents	Older couples	Older single people	Pensioners	Total
Consumerism	5	2	2	1	1	11
Ups and downs	3	2	2	1	1	9
Managing bills	1	0	1	1	8	11
Total	9	4	5	3	10	31

KEY POINTS

- New customers are recruited through personal recommendation, advertising and the canvassing of goods.

- Moneylenders are not recklessly taking on new customers who cannot afford their loans. Most new customers are in work and are not borrowing out of desperation.

- Customers' situations change and some people subsequently use moneylending as a way of financing basic expenditure such as bill-paying.

4   The Reasons Why People Use Moneylenders

The costs of credit from a moneylender are much higher than for other types of credit so why do so many people use it? It could be because these people are desperate for money and have limited choice to other types of credit. And they may not understand quite how much more expensive moneylending is. We saw in the last chapter that when people first became customers of a moneylender they were not generally in dire financial straits although their situations did sometimes deteriorate. This chapter assesses why people used moneylending rather than other, cheaper types of credit. The chapter also discusses the advantages as well as the disadvantages of using a moneylender.

As well as looking at how much choice people had in using a moneylender, this chapter investigates whether use of a moneylender was a rational decision. Critics might argue that, because of the very high APRs, people must be making an irrational choice to use a moneylender. The argument is that if someone is relatively affluent, they would be better off using a cheaper form of credit. If they are relatively poor, then they are making themselves even poorer by using a moneylender and so should desist from doing so. Implicit in this is the view that those who do use a moneylender must be doing so either because they do not know enough about the cost of this type of credit and the alternatives available or because they are poor money managers and are unable to make sensible decisions. Concern also arises about the amount of pressure put on people to use a moneylender when they do not really wish to do so.

Becoming a customer
The more long-standing customers who had become customers in the decade or two following the second world war would not have had

many credit alternatives. Those were the days before the expansion in the credit industry which began in the late 1960s. There were nine people who had become customers before 1970. Most of these had bought goods, such as children's shoes and clothes, and then paid for them in instalments over the following weeks. Tallymen, clothing clubs and check-trading have been a long-established part of working class life. 'Granny' bought 'mum's' clothes in this way. 'Mum' bought her clothes in this way and now this customer, herself, would buy clothes for her own children in this way. It was often seen as the only way of being able to buy such essentials.

But, even if there were no credit alternatives, why didn't these people save their money and then buy the necessary items? While it would have been interesting to have explored this area with some of the more long-standing customers, this would have meant asking them to recall details of their financial situations and attitudes going back almost half a century in some cases. Although studies using oral history do explore such issues, this study is rooted more in the situation today and so the issues around saving have been explored through customers' current situations. Other studies have documented the realities of working class life in the earlier part of this century (see for example, Pember Reeves 1979).

The 31 customers interviewed became customers of a moneylender in one of three ways. More than half had identified a need and then considered, to a greater or lesser extent, the options available to them before deciding to borrow from a moneylender. About a quarter were encouraged by a canvasser to identify a need and then told that they could satisfy this need by buying from the canvasser on credit. And a fifth were aware that they were eligible for credit from a moneylender, decided to take advantage of that option and then considered how they would use the available credit.

Identifying a need and considering alternatives
More than half (17) of all customers interviewed had first decided to borrow from a moneylender because they had identified a particular purchase which they wished to make and, to some extent, considered the alternatives. The amount of choice open to them depended on three factors: their income level, the reason for borrowing and their knowledge of different credit options.

Most of them would probably have had some difficulty getting credit from other sources. Those who were still living at home were on relatively low incomes and would probably be fairly unattractive to other lenders. Those in couples with small children were often in council accommodation and although one partner usually had a job, this was often in relatively low-paid and insecure work. Those who had turned to a moneylender when in difficulties would certainly have found it hard to borrow from other lenders.

But there was little evidence of people applying for other types of credit and being turned down. Most people ruled out alternative sources for one or more of four reasons: they felt that they would be turned down and so did not bother applying; they preferred cash budgets and feared using credit cards or overdrafts; they felt that other sources were unsuitable for their needs; or they were so unfamiliar with other sources that they did not even consider them.

For some people, particularly men, being turned down for credit was seen as a blow to their self-esteem. This was because it either reflected the fact that they could not afford the credit they had applied for or they were not trusted to pay it back. Either way, there was a stigma attached to being rejected and so people preferred to use a familiar source that they knew was open to them. So people were reluctant to apply for mainstream credit if they feared there was a chance of rejection, and given their circumstances, the chances of rejection were pretty high. The lack of a formal application process also meant that if a moneylender did want to turn them down they could do so informally and with subtlety rather than sending them a rejection letter.

Earlier research has shown that some people living on very low incomes prefer to operate cash budgets and, when they need to borrow money, prefer to use a moneylender rather than run the risk of over-spending on credit cards or use an overdraft facility (Kempson 1994).

One couple were committed to cash and would not consider using a bank account, a cheque book or credit cards,

> *People do believe in them for convenience. But I think you can get in too much [debt]. If you limit yourself it's OK, but I like cash.*

Concern about being in control of money was reflected in the view that people should only use one source of credit at a time. One customer explained that she did not use any other types of credit or any other moneylending companies because,

> *I just didn't want to get myself into too much debt.*

Using a moneylender was often seen as a way of managing cash rather than using credit. So people who disliked 'credit' felt quite happy to use moneylending. As one woman explained,

> *He won't have any credit cards, he won't have anything on HP. If he wants something he likes to pay for it there and then, so he hasn't got to think that's got to be paid for.*

Another reason why people were reluctant to use other types of credit was that it was often thought unsuitable for their needs. For example, one couple, with four young children had both been in work when they first used a moneylender. They wanted the money to help pay some bills that they had received. They only wanted a relatively small amount of money – a couple of hundred pounds – and knew that a bank or building society were unlikely to lend such a small sum, particularly if they knew what it was for. They might have been able to get credit cards, but they did not want to have them, preferring to deal in cash. For this couple there was an element of choice in their decision to go to the moneylender.

Another reason for not favouring alternative sources of credit was lack of familiarity with them. Twelve of the seventeen who had identified a need had close friends or family who used the moneylender. So they were generally aware of the pros and cons of using a moneylender before they became customers. Other sources of credit were much less familiar. Would they be given a credit card or turned down? What would happen if they got a credit card? Would they start spending recklessly? How would a bank manager look at them? A study by the National Consumer Council showed that some people had a fear of bank managers which made it difficult to approach them (NCC 1983). One customer from the NCC study said,

> *I think bank managers are frightening people; I don't like going to see mine at all. He seems to sit up at the other side of the desk and never smiles and makes me feel as though I'm begging for money. I just hate it.*

Moneylenders were much more familiar to many people than bank managers.

For most people, other forms of credit were either unavailable or unsuitable so they had little choice except, perhaps, to save or go without. But it would be patronising to say that people should have gone without some things or tried harder to save. Those on a low income generally found it difficult to save because there were always many calls on their money. One of the advantages of a moneylender, as we shall see later, was that the timing and reliability of the weekly knock on the door meant that people had a good chance of paying their weekly amount and therefore keeping open their access to this form of credit. For some, using a moneylender was almost a method of saving. Indeed, over time, as one loan replaced another, it could easily be thought that weekly payments were saving towards a future amount of money coming in rather than repayments for a past loan. People were aware that they were paying high interest for their loans but were prepared to do so in order that they could have what they wanted now rather than go without.

Where people identified a need and then decided how to meet that need it is relatively straightforward to measure the amount of choice and constraint facing them.

For example, a lone mother wished to decorate her home and neither had enough money saved nor enough in her current income to cover the cost. She could have postponed the decoration until she had saved up for it but she found it difficult to save and she had grown tired of the current condition of her home. She wanted the money now. Her family might have been able to lend her some of the money but they did not have much and she did not want to ask because she wanted to maintain her independence. She decided to borrow the money. As a lone parent she knew that she would have some difficulty borrowing from a bank or building society. And in any case she only wanted one hundred pounds. She did not have a credit card and did not want one because of fear of debt. Her brother had used a moneylending firm in the past and was happy with the service. She asked her brother to get the same collector to visit her and she took out a loan. She knew that the interest rate was high but was prepared to pay for it in order to improve her living conditions.

This woman faced a choice between using a moneylender or trying to save up for redecoration. She chose to use the moneylender.

The question remains as to whether these people were acting rationally. Economists would use rational choice theory to evaluate the decisions made by consumers. This theory, in its crudest neoclassical form, is often criticised by sociologists for assuming perfect information, the primacy of financial costs/benefits and stable preferences. Subjective expected utility theory developed in response to this. As Esser notes, its basic idea is that,

> *from a set of feasible alternatives, persons choose that course of action that seems most likely to realise highly valued goals, given the structure of the decision situation. (Esser 1993)*

According to this version of rational choice theory, we can say that the moneylender customers did indeed act rationally since they chose between available and suitable alternatives to achieve particular goals.

But not all decisions to borrow begin with the consumer independently identifying a need.

Canvassers encouraging people to borrow

In a quarter of cases (8), it was canvassers who encouraged people to borrow. As we have seen, canvassers were employed to knock on people's doors and try to persuade them that what they really need is a first-aid kit or a duvet set or some gold earrings. Some people agree that they need these items and so want to buy them. The canvasser then mentions that they can be bought for a certain sum every week. The consumer agrees and so, somewhat indirectly, becomes the customer of a moneylender. In these cases, it is not that people need credit and therefore turn to a moneylender, it is that they want a particular good which the moneylender sells and they therefore buy it using this source of credit.

The amount of choice in such a case is open to debate. Canvassers were not observed as part of this study and so it is difficult to say what techniques they used. Certainly some moneylending customers mentioned that they had experience of pushy sales reps coming to their doors. Most of these were resisted. But perhaps others used more subtle techniques? Other studies have shown how canvassers, or 'peddlers' as they were still referred to in the United States, are successful in encouraging people to buy goods. As David Caplovitz remarked,

> *By calling on the housewife, frequently when the husband is not at home, the peddler is able to break down many of the usual constraints upon consumption ... By bringing his goods to the door and offering easy credit, the peddler, in effect, elevates the housewife to the role*

of the major consumer, activating whatever impulses she may have to buy. (Caplovitz 1967)

This kind of impulse-buying involved relatively little conscious decision-making. Customers did not consider alternative sources of credit in such situations. Those interviewed who had bought on impulse were generally pleased with what they had bought. But this could have been a form of post-hoc rationalisation. It is true, however, that most of these purchases were fairly small-scale – often around £50. Although this could be quite a lot to someone on a low income, the small weekly repayments were generally manageable. It would be easy to say that people should know better than to buy on impulse, but this type of purchasing is probably just as common, if not more so, among high-income consumers. We might argue that the side-effects are more dangerous for low-income consumers – in terms of possible increased hardship – but the low level of repayments suggest that such side-effects would be fairly small and short-lived.

Following in the family tradition
In the remaining fifth of cases (6), people started using credit from a moneylender simply because it was available. These young people had seen others in their families use the moneylender and associated it with providing an extra source of money. As soon as they had established themselves in a job, they decided to ask for a loan. Then they considered what they could buy with it. As with those canvassed, these new customers did not consider alternative sources of credit.

It could be argued that this type of decision-making is not rational because it does not start with identifying a goal and choosing between feasible alternatives, as is necessary for subjective expected utility theory to hold. The interpretative sociologist, Alfred Schutz has argued that such a theory is at odds with the reality of everyday life, where people act more in accordance with tradition and routine than conscious, individual calculation (Schultz 1964). But Esser argues that although people's decisions may owe more to routine and habit than conscious calculation, this does not mean that they are irrational. This is because there are good reasons for people to follow traditions and routines which have had positive outcomes for other people in similar situations. Any alternative action would incur great costs in terms of the time needed to acquire information and the risk associated with trying out something unusual. The costs and risks involved with embarking on an alternative course therefore make it rational to continue with a familiar course. As Esser notes,

> *Routines are satisfactory and relatively cheap solutions of typical problems in daily life ... there is thus something like a steeply decreasing marginal utility of additional information in the presence of already proved routines.*

So if one member of the family has borrowed from a moneylender without any great problems, then the member of the next generation, who is in a similar situation, is making a rational decision to follow in the family tradition.

Deciding to borrow from a particular company

The moneylending industry acknowledges that most of its customers have limited access to alternative sources of credit. But they argue that there is competition between moneylending companies which keeps the costs of credit down and increases the amount of choice facing prospective customers. But once again, the role of security, habit and family tradition acts as a disincentive for customers to shop around.

Most of those who identified a need and then decided to borrow from a moneylender used a company that has been used by friends or family. This was a safe option. The operation of the company and the personality of the collector were known and so the new customer had less to worry about. Even if their friend or relative thought that there were drawbacks to using them, they at least knew what the drawbacks were. A completely new company might promise a better deal, but could they be trusted? As various customers said, *'better the devil you know'*. One woman was prepared to pay more for the security of doing business with a well established company,

> *[The company] are one of the most well known. I mean everyone knows that their interest rates are higher than the average, but I'd rather go to them than go to someone out of the paper you don't know.*

Five people did not know companies or collectors through family or friends. They saw the company advertised and so took the risk of calling them. One woman only knew about moneylending through what she had picked up from the media. She was very scared at first that she might be contacting a loanshark. As she explained,

> *I was very frightened about doing it, you know, I thought, 'Is this right?' because I'd heard so much about these financial companies*

lending money but I thought I'd give it a go ... There's the old saying that there are sharks that don't come up to expectation and keep on asking you to take out another loan and I was afraid that they'd start pressuring me.

Those who borrowed from canvassers did not necessarily know the company or the collector that would eventually call on them. But with the small sums of money which were usually involved, the risk of dealing with a new company seemed slight and, again, there was little consideration of alternatives.

Those who followed the family tradition automatically used the family company and collector.

Although tradition and security tend to limit the amount that people will shop around, families and friends often have experience of more than one company and so new customer did have some choice between a couple of familiar companies.

So there was some choice between different companies, but generally customers were very conservative and tended to start and stay with the company they knew rather than risk someone unfamiliar.

Although this section has considered the choice open to customers in a general way, the next section of this chapter discusses each of the possible alternative types of credit in more detail.

The alternatives to using moneylender

Although most people only used credit from the moneylender, some had used or were currently using other sources. One of the main indicators of access to and use of mainstream credit is possession of a bank or building society account with a cheque facility (Kempson 1994). About half of all customers had such a facility.

Nine people were currently using other forms of credit. Seven of these were using mail order only. One was using mail order and had credit cards and a bank overdraft arrangement. One was only using credit cards and an overdraft. The two with credit cards and overdrafts were only using them sparingly.

Eleven had used other types of credit in the past but were not doing so now. Again, most of these (9) had used a mail order catalogue but five had previously had a bank or building society loan. Three had used HP, two had had credit cards and one had received a loan from the social fund.

The remaining eleven customers had never used other types of credit.

Bank/building society loans

Most people would not have been able to secure loans from banks or building societies even if they wanted to. Their relatively low incomes and job insecurity would have made them unattractive to these mainstream lenders. Council tenancy would also have counted against them in application scoring. But even if bank or building society loans had been available, they would probably not have been suitable, as borrowers usually wanted small loans which they could repay weekly.

Two people had actually been turned down for bank or building society loans. One man had just left the army after being posted in West Germany. He needed some money to re-establish himself in this country. He had a job lined up for himself but there was a period in between when he had no work. He applied to a building society for a loan but was turned down and so went to a moneylending company instead. This man was very much the exception rather than the rule as there was little evidence that others had tried to get other types of credit and been turned down.

The other was a young woman who had applied when she was single and in work. She was now a lone parent and knew that if she could not get a loan while in work, there was no way that she would get one now. She, like others who had not even applied for such loans, was critical of the number of forms she had had to fill in and the amount of time she had had to wait before finding out that her application was unsuccessful.

Some had not applied for a loan because they suspected they would be turned down. Some did not even consider applying loan because they preferred to deal in cash or knew that a bank loan would have to be for a large amount of money with large monthly repayments. Some of the older couples had always used cash. They would not have been eligible for a loan without an account. When she was asked if she had a bank or building society account, one 70 year-old woman only considered the answer in terms of her husband,

> *No I don't think he uses a bank. He's got his own bank – his own box upstairs, so he does it that way.*

But even some younger people had not really considered using a bank. One woman in her late thirties said,

> *No, we've never dealt with banks. We have got a building society account what his wages are paid into, but we've never had banks. I*

don't know why, we've just never, I don't know. I've never thought about it really. I don't know really.

Another woman had only considered using a bank because her sister had told her she ought to. She said,

My sister will say to me, 'I don't know why you bother with [the moneylender]. Why don't you get the loan through the bank?' and all this. I suppose it's just what you get used to. I'm so used to having [the moneylender]. It just wouldn't dawn on me to sort of run them down and go with the bank.

Others had had bank or building society loans in the past. In most cases, such loans are cheaper than borrowing from moneylenders. But one couple found that they were charged heavily for missing payments,

We have had a bank loan a couple of years ago now. And it was awful. We were paying about £80 a month it was, which we are paying now. But if we left it one month, we used to get a letter and then they'd add another 25 quid onto that and interest on if you don't pay it. And in the end you're paying double what you originally got. It was horrifying.

Another couple had taken out a bank loan to buy their disabled daughter a computer which had been designed for someone with her impairment. The computer was very expensive and the couple were paying £130 a month for four years. They found this amount of money extremely difficult to find. And they also disliked having a large loan hanging over them for four years. In contrast, loans from moneylenders were of shorter duration and lower weekly repayments, even if they were more expensive. The couple had borrowed from the bank because they needed a large sum and knew that it would be cheaper than borrowing from the moneylender.

A third couple had taken out a bank loan to pay for a car and to pay off their poll tax arrears. They repaid the loan through direct debit. They went to the bank because it was a relatively large sum and the interest was lower than it would have been through a moneylender. They only used the moneylender to buy hampers, rent their TV and buy very small amounts of vouchers.

Overdrafts

As we have seen, some people believed in using cash alone. They did not have bank or building society accounts and so could not use an overdraft facility. But some people had gone overdrawn in the past and had been charged heavily for the 'privilege'. Although an authorised overdraft would not incur such charges, many people on low incomes are unable to get authorization to go overdrawn (Kempson 1994). The charges associated with unauthorised overdrafts can be extortionate. As one young woman explained,

> *We were overdrawn on our overdraft by £2.19 and the bank charged us £59 and I wrote them a letter ... and they apologised and said they would overlook it this time. It was crazy.*

Although this woman was very angry about the charge, she did say that she would always use her overdraft or her credit cards in preference to borrowing cash from a moneylender because she thought that the interest rates would be much lower with such facilities. She only used the moneylending company to buy goods.

Credit cards

If some people were sceptical about using banks or building societies to obtain credit, no-one had a good word to say about credit cards. The vast majority had never had credit cards and had no intention of ever applying for them. Most feared the possibility of overspending with them. In some senses, credit cards are to working class people what moneylenders are to middle class people. They are unfamiliar and seen as likely to encourage overspending and trap people in a cycle of uncontrollable debt.

One woman in her early 60s explained,

> *One thing I wouldn't have is credit cards ... I think they get people into debt, they do ... I think people go mad sometimes. If I want a thing I'll save up for what I want, you know, then I'll buy it. But I wouldn't have these cards. I go mad at my daughter because she's got a card.*

A woman in her 30s had a similar opinion,

> *I don't like credit cards. I've heard some people, a lot of people getting into trouble with them ... They just go out and spend on them, don't they, don't think about what they've got to pay back. I wouldn't have one, no.*

One young woman had been sent a card but said that it was,

> *Too much trouble. They sent me one but I just cut it up. Better not to get involved at all.*

Only three people had ever used credit cards and none were currently using them. One couple had used credit cards and had got into debt with them,

> *I run amuck on them so I wouldn't do it again. It was too easy to go out and when you wanted to get something and use them so I paid them off and cut them up, paid them off and wouldn't have a credit card again.*

Another couple had also got into debt after a family crisis. The credit card company was very unsympathetic and they had stopped using their card altogether. But they said that they would use the card sensibly in the future.

So credit cards were rarely considered by borrowers to be an acceptable or suitable form of credit. But even if these people had wanted to use credit cards, it is unlikely that many would have reached the 'pass mark' on any application scoring exercise. Contrary to their popular image, credit card companies do not issue cards to anyone who applies – a recent study of credit card use reported that one major company rejected 40 per cent of new applicants (Rowlingson and Kempson 1994). And those people who had defaulted on their credit cards had seen dramatic downturns in their financial situations since they first had cards.

Mail order catalogues

If credit cards were the unacceptable face of credit, mail order catalogues were the reverse. Most people had either used them in the past or were currently doing so. Of course, credit from catalogues was only linked to goods and so people who borrowed money to repay bills or buy things which could not be bought through a catalogue would not find them a viable alternative to other sources of credit.

Catalogues were used because they were convenient, gave a wide choice of goods and had no interest added to the price. Where the mail order agent was a friend, catalogues had all the advantages of weekly doorstep collection.

But there were also several disadvantages of using a catalogue. The goods were often considered expensive and would be cheaper in a market or in some shops. This may well be because the cost of credit has been buried in the cash price. As a woman in her 60s said,

> *If you can go down the town you can get the same stuff a lot cheaper down the road, be far better really. You could have a loan even for*

> *that, get a loan and then go down the town and get the stuff about*
> *quarter as cheap.*

The goods could not be seen and inspected and it was awkward to send them back if they were not liked. Forms had to be filled in and there was quite a time lag between ordering and receiving goods. Payment could be weekly, but this could involve inconvenience if the money had to be sent off or paid into a bank or post office. And there was concern that such methods of payment might be forgotten leading to debt.

One customer saw the pros and cons of using mail order catalogues which is why she borrowed from a moneylender at the same time as using a catalogue,

> *Things are quite a lot dearer in a catalogue comparing with a shop.*
> *Sometimes it can be, like on games and things for children. For*
> *example, some can be as much as £5 difference. I suppose if you're*
> *borrowing [from a moneylender], you're still paying interest on that*
> *and I suppose it maybe it balances itself out that way, but I do both.*

HP from a shop

Some people had used HP to buy large items like three-piece suites and electrical equipment. One woman considered buying a carpet on HP but then decided to buy a carpet direct from the moneylender's company. She thought it was good quality and a fair price. Also, her partner rarely went shopping with her and the only way she could get his agreement to buy the carpet was when he saw the sample brought round by the moneylender.

One woman had bought her TV and video on interest free credit with an electrical store but she had then bought a CD through the moneylending company. She realised that she was paying more in interest by using the moneylender rather than getting HP, but she preferred to pay weekly as she did not miss the money that way,

> *I would have noticed the £20 or whatever a month. Actually when I*
> *think about it, I'm paying [the equivalent of] £28 a month, but my*
> *husband gets paid every Thursday and I always put my bill money*
> *aside and I get paid on a Friday so I don't miss the £7 [a week].*

One family had tried to buy a TV on credit in a store but were turned down. So they decided instead to rent a TV from the moneylender's company. Several people rented their TVs in this way. It was seen as expensive, but repairs were free and there was a slot machine so that people could pay as they watched rather than having to find the money every month. Some people asked their machine to be set at a high rate so that they could save money through the TV and have a rebate when the slot was emptied.

The social fund

The social fund is a cash-limited government fund which offers loans and some grants to benefit claimants for the purchase of urgently-needed items, such as beds, cookers and clothing. It replaced a previous system of 'single payment' grants which were not cash-limited. To get a loan, most people have to be receiving income support. One of the main criticisms of the social fund is that there is no difference in need between those who receive such loans and those who apply and are rejected (Huby and Dix 1992). But in spite of all the evidence, the government has so far refused to reform the social fund because while it is clearly not achieving its aim of targeting resources on those in most need it is meeting its aim of saving government money (Berthoud 1991).

Most of the people interviewed would not have been eligible for a social fund loan because they were not receiving income support. Indeed, few people had even heard of the social fund. Those who had heard of it generally knew very little about it and only a few had considered applying for money from it. One woman who was currently receiving invalidity benefit had learnt about the social fund because her daughter had received a loan through it. She thought it was a very good idea because the loans were interest free, but she was not receiving income support and so knew that she would have difficulty getting one.

One of the lone parents had received a loan from the social fund in the past. She thought that,

> *It was good in the respect that it had no interest. What you borrowed was what you paid back. So it was very quick to finish.*

But there were drawbacks,

> *There was a lot of paperwork. They ask a lot of questions – hassle. If I didn't need it then I wouldn't have done it.*

The social fund was tapped when she was desperate. In other circumstances, she used the moneylender because although she had to pay interest, it was a much simpler, quicker and less intrusive way of getting a loan. In any case, the last loan that she had taken out from the moneylender had been for a camcorder. She would definitely not have been given a social fund loan to buy such an item.

Credit unions

Because of the various criticisms of moneylending, many policy-makers and welfare agencies have advocated the development of credit unions as an alternative source of credit for low-income groups.

Credit unions in this country have their origins in the friendly societies of the 19th century. They are self-help organisations run mainly by volunteers. Members, who must be united by a 'common bond', can save up to £5,000 and can borrow up to £5,000 plus the amount of their savings. The rate of interest is fixed at 1% per month. The development of credit unions in the UK has not been as successful as has been the case in North America and Ireland. Only one in 300 adults in Britain are members of a credit union. And there are only about 400 unions in existence at the moment.

PSI research into credit unions found that members were principally attracted to the opportunity to save rather than borrow (Berthoud and Hinton 1989). And once savings were taken into account there was not much difference in the cost of borrowing from a credit union compared with a bank or building society. Members also tended to use mid- and up-market credit sources at the same time as belonging to the credit union. They did not come from the poorer sections of the community. A report by the National Consumer Council suggested that credit unions faced various barriers to expansion such as the lack of common bonds and the need for training, better premises and equipment. Low awareness of credit unions was also highlighted (NCC 1994). A recent report from the Association of Metropolitan Authorities argued that current funding of credit unions by local councils may be reduced as a consequence of government cuts making expansion even more difficult (AMA 1994).

None of the people interviewed were using a credit union. On the round which took place entirely on one large council estate there was an established credit union at the local school. Of the four people interviewed on this estate, one had not heard of the credit union. Another was aware that there was one, but knew nothing further about it. One knew a surprising amount about the credit union, but what he did know discouraged him from using it,

> *I've seen it advertised. I haven't bothered to ask how it works but if you do [use it] you'd have to get rid of [one of the two moneylenders he used] because you'd be paying another £10 a week out or whatever you'd agreed to, I believe. But from what I can gather, if we went into it we could say pay them £10 a week for 10 weeks. On the 10th week they'd give us £100 loan. And it's only our money that we've paid in anyway. But instead of paying £140 back, you only pay £110 or £120 back. You're paying an awful lot less money back, but you've already paid the money in. So the way I look on that is, if I've paid £100 in already and I'm having £100 back out, which is my £100 anyway, I might as well have a bank account because I'm paying £20 interest on my £100 ... that's what I can't gather about it!*

This man obviously knew that it was cheaper to borrow from a credit union. But he was confused by the fact that borrowers had to first of all save with the credit union. He could not see why this made the credit union any different from having a savings account. What he did not realise was that people can borrow more from a credit union than they put in, so it is different from having a bank or building society savings account. But the difficulty of saving in the first place was a barrier to joining a credit union.

The third person who knew about the local credit union was also averse to using it. This was because she did not want the parents at the local school to know that she needed loans: *'they'd all gossip and that'*. She preferred the relative privacy of having a caller visit the house every week.

Borrowing from family or friends
Poor people tend to come from poor families, have poor friends and live in poor neighbourhoods. But even so, there is a great deal of informal support both within and between families (Kempson et al 1994). Where people do use support from their families, there is usually a desire to ensure that such help is reciprocated. If support is in one direction only, this is seen as dependence and most people try hard to avoid becoming dependent on family or friends. Borrowing from a moneylender is sometimes one way of avoiding informal borrowing. To preserve her relationship with her daughters, a divorcee

had started using a moneylender. She was keen for her children not to find out that she had done so,

> *I'd rather they didn't know because then they would want to take over all my bills and I don't think it's fair on them ... I can imagine they'll say, 'oh, you shouldn't have anything to do with them – they're moneylenders'. In a sense that's the old-fashioned word, 'moneylender', and I think they'd be really upset. I do occasionally get a cheque from them, mostly birthdays and Christmas ... We've got such a great relationship between the three of us ... and I wouldn't want that to disappear.*

Saving or going without

People may not be able to use other types of credit or they may believe that moneylending is the most suitable type for them at a particular time. But do they need to use credit at all? Wouldn't it be better for them to save up for what they want? Or go without it?

As far as delaying a purchase goes, people at all income levels are prepared to pay extra in order to have something today rather than, say, in three months time. Several people said that if they had not got the loan they would have just saved up and got what they wanted later, but they preferred to pay more and have it sooner. As one woman said of her partner,

> *He believes in saving and saving. But you can wait forever! You know what women are like – they like to buy things.*

Some people said that they would not have been able to save for what they wanted. As they were on a low income there was always something which would seem worth buying rather than putting the money away. One woman borrowed £700 a year to go on holiday. This cost her £21 a week. If she had been able to save the money, she would only have needed to put away about £15 a week, but she knew that she would end up spending that money each week if it wasn't for the thought that a collector would be calling to pick it up.

As another woman explained,

> *I can't save, that's what's the matter with me ... if we've got something saved, we dip into it, so it's easier to borrow and then you've got to pay it back.*

One mother had six children and found that if she had any money left over at the end of the week there was always a claim on it from at least one of them.

Another customer remarked,

> *It's too easy to spend if he doesn't come for it. I don't know, something comes up. You think, 'oh I'll leave it and I'll make it up'. It's not easy to make up. At least if he comes for it, you're sure it's there which is important.*

Others said that their lack of ability to save was not a result of poverty but because they just could not put money by and spent whatever they had. As one customer said,

> *I often say to myself, 'oh, I'll finish with [my collector] and not bother any more.' But the money would just go.*

One customer said that the amount they paid to their collector was so small that they did not notice it and so would easily spend it if the collector did not take it.

If people needed money for an essential item, such as a bill which had to be paid, then there was little time to save and people were forced to pay the extra to avoid getting into arrears.

One couple did have savings, but they preferred to keep their savings for an emergency and were reluctant to dip into it for anything else in case they never replaced the money borrowed. They also took into account the fact that they would lose interest on their savings, even though this would have been much less than that paid to the moneylender. One of them realised that they,

> *could draw money out of our savings, but it won't go back again. But when [the collector] comes, I know he's going to take £25 and I don't miss it. And if I draw money out of my savings, I'm losing interest.*

So people generally could have gone without or tried to save up for what they wanted but they preferred to pay extra and get what they wanted immediately. There were four main reasons for this: some felt that they could have saved but simply did not want to wait for consumer goods, some found it very difficult to save, some needed money for an emergency and others wanted to keep their savings – if they had any – for a rainy day.

The pros and cons of using a moneylender

As we have seen, most of the people interviewed had limited access to other forms of credit. This was partly because they came from groups which many creditors were not keen to lend to. It was also because other forms of credit were not suitable, often involving large sums of money with large monthly repayments. Credit from a moneylender, on the other hand, was much more suitable and so had more advantages than using other forms of credit.

It is important to remember when reading this section, that the people interviewed were all current customers of moneylenders. It is therefore likely that they will mention many positive aspects of the service as a way of justifying their current actions. It is also likely that those who have found that the disadvantages outweigh the advantages no longer borrow from this source.

The advantages of using a moneylender

Customers liked being able to borrow relatively small amounts of money and repay them weekly. When asked how he would feel about paying monthly, one customer explained,

> *Because I'm paid weekly it would work out difficult for me because I'd have to put my money away each week ... it would be hell, you know. It's alright if you're paid monthly isn't it? But if you're not it would be a bit of a bugbear.*

The stereotypical view of a moneylender's customer is someone who is deep in debt and out of control with their finances. This may happen in some cases, but many customers used a moneylender precisely because they were very keen to keep control over their money and not get into debt. They felt that there was less risk of getting into serious debt with a moneylender than there would be if they were using other forms of credit such as credit cards. This was because they knew that the knock on the door would come every week and they would repay their loan. If they had to send the money off every week or pay it into a bank, there was much more chance that they would fall behind with their repayments. One customer explained that if moneylending did not exist she knew that she would spend all her money and get into debt, as she had done before,

> *[My money] would just fritter away. I've got to really have control over money because I can be reckless ... this is the one thing I dread – not being able to pay my bills ... [but] I don't dread now getting into debt. I feel that through him I can control my spending.*

Another customer pointed directly to the advantages of doorstep collection,

> *The convenience of having someone call here ... you know you can't leave it because you know somebody's going to call. And personally I think that's probably how a lot of people do get into debt because they know, 'oh, no-one's going to come knocking on my door, so we can leave it for another week,' and it just builds up. Because someone's knocking on the door, you know, you've got to have the money there and it does make it a lot easier. It's a bit like the old rent collector, isn't it? I mean, they didn't have the arrears with the old rent collectors.*

This customer's view is reinforced by research which has shown that one of the factors relating to rent arrears is method of collection (Duncan and Kirby 1983). Doorstep collection is related to much lower arrears than payment at the post office. But the costs of doorstep collection along with the risk of theft and violence has encouraged local authorities to discontinue the practice. The proportion of council tenants who had their rent collected personally dropped from 42% in 1981 to 19% in 1989 (Berthoud and Kempson 1992).

Other customers also preferred doorstep collection. One had previously had a bank loan but preferred borrowing from the moneylender,

> *With [the collector] coming round, you know she's coming round, so you know you've got to put it away for her because she's coming round. It's also that bit embarrassing as well when you open the door and sort of say, 'I can't afford to pay it this week' whereas with the bank you don't see them ... you think, 'I've got to go to the bank' but you tend to spend it.*

When asked what she would do if the moneylending company decided to ask customers to pay by paying at a post office or sending their money, another customer replied,

> *I wouldn't do it, so they wouldn't get it so regularly. It's a pain isn't it? I think that's probably why I prefer somebody calling to the door than a catalogue. Because you know that you're going to be here at a certain time and a certain day and, you know, you can almost tell the time by [the collector].*

One customer preferred to buy her hampers from the moneylending firm rather than from the man who delivered the milk,

> *They was bigger and better and .. with our milkman, sometimes he doesn't even call every week for his money. If he hasn't got time he just drives past and calls for it on a Monday or whatever. Well*

Mondays you haven't always got the money ... but [the collector] you can pay weekly and it's all finished by Christmas.

One customer summed up the benefits of doorstep collection,

You pay far quicker, easier and better if they come round.

The personal call was mainly appreciated because it ensured that repayments were kept to. But it was also much more convenient than having to make a special trip to pay instalments in another way. This was particularly welcomed by women with several young children. One young mother, whose own mother had used the same collector said,

I'd rather have someone I know rather than traipsing round post offices and banks paying in. So he was more convenient and I knew him before so I trusted him in that way, so I was quite happy.

Older or disabled people who had mobility problems also appreciated personal collection. One woman had had problems with her knee and was unable to get about much. As well as the practical difficulties that she would have had in getting out to pay or post any credit instalments, she also appreciated the personal contact with the collector as she lived on her own.

Coming through much of this material is an interesting attitude towards credit, debt and default. For some people, credit is synonymous with debt, because money is owed. For others, debt is only where an agreement to pay is broken, whether that be an agreement to pay rent, a gas bill or a credit arrangement. So for some people, using credit is a way of staying out of debt because it allows them to have some control and certainty about their money. They know that, as long as they keep up their repayments, they will have a certain amount of money coming to them every few months. This money can then be used to pay any bills and keep out of debt. As one customer put it,

If I didn't have a loan, I'd always be in debt!

Another of the advantages of using a moneylender was that it was relatively easy to get credit. There were few large forms to fill in and a relatively short amount of time to wait. As one customer remarked,

You can ask them for a loan on the Friday and they'll be out here by the Monday ... and they'll give it you that day, it's convenient.

Someone else expressed a similar view,

> *It's only a phone call away and he always comes, very good. We don't have to wait sort of seven days for this, for approval and all that. He'll come back to you virtually the following day. He'll ring you at work or wherever and say, 'yeah, that's fine. When do you want me to call?*

As well as being easy to get credit, customers thought the system was easy to understand. This was partly because their families had used the system in the past. But it was also because the moneylenders stressed the amount borrowed, the amount to be repaid, the weekly instalments and the length of the loan. Customers knew that the interest was high, but as long as they could afford the weekly repayments, they were less concerned with the interest.

Most people were aware that the interest rate was higher than most sources of credit. But customers were also aware that other forms of credit levied default charges if someone missed an instalment. With moneylending, people could miss payments and take longer to pay than originally agreed and would not have to pay a penny more than the original sum they had promised to repay. This actually meant that the real interest rate was lower than the contractually-stated rate because they did not have to pay an extra charge. As one customer explained,

> *You do pay a lot more interest on the [moneylender] than you did with the bank, but then ... if you can't afford to pay you don't get the interest added on anyway which you do for the bank.*

So although the interest rates were seen as a disadvantage, this disadvantage was not always as great as it looked on paper.

Another advantage of using a moneylender, mentioned earlier, was its familiarity. It has already been shown that people tend to follow in the family tradition when borrowing from a moneylender. One woman echoed the views of many when she said,

> *The devil you know is better than the devil you don't!*

People disliked borrowing from most sources of credit but at least they understood the system of credit from a moneylender. And if the collector had been known to the family for some time, they could be sure that he or she would continue to provide a reasonable service. When people have little spare cash it is understandable that they might be very cautious with it and be wary of trying out new forms of credit.

The disadvantages of using a moneylender

By far the main disadvantage, mentioned by customers, was the level of interest on loans. But many people were not aware and not particularly concerned about the APR. Their views were based more on the proportion of money they were repaying on top of the principal amount. This calculation was made regardless of the time period of the loan. For example, one man said that he borrowed £100 and was charged £20. He was quite happy with this, saying that it was only 20 per cent interest. If the loan had been over 16 weeks, a fairly typical time-scale, the APR on this loan would have been 200 per cent rather than 20 per cent. Although APRs have their limitations in providing a comparable measure of the costs of credit, they are the best available measure and are certainly more accurate than the calculation resorted to by most customers.

One company was extremely open about the details of their loans, including the APR. It printed its ready-reckoner tables on customers' weekly payment cards. This gave details of the following: the different amounts that could be borrowed, the charge for borrowing that amount, the total repayable, the weekly payment and the number of weeks over which the loan had to be paid. The APR was also shown. Customers of other companies would have had to look hard to find the APR if they had wanted to know what it was. At the time of taking out a loan, the agent would write into their payment cards the following: the amount borrowed, the charge, the total payable, the weekly payment and the period over which it was borrowed. The APR would not be written down in the payment book as a matter of course.

But even without this information, most people, unlike the man mentioned above, knew that the interest they were paying was very high. One customer said that it was, *'sky high'*. Another regularly took out cash loans and then used the money to shop around for the best deals on goods in town. He was prepared to pay the interest on these loans, but when he saw the amount of interest put on goods he was not so happy,

> *I asked them to bring me a duvet cover. Of course when he brought it they hadn't took me interest ticket off it ... and I turned round and said, 'I ain't paying for that, I'm not having that,' he says, 'why?' I said, 'because ... I ain't paying that much interest on it when I can get it cheaper.' And he took it back and I never heard no more from him.*

This reaction is surprising given that interest on cash loans was invariably higher than that on goods. Some people said that they would only buy goods from the moneylender because cash loans were so expensive. This man accepted a high rate of interest on cash but could not bring himself to buy an item which he knew he could get a lot cheaper elsewhere.

Other people were prepared to pay the extra because they could only afford to buy something with the help of credit. As one customer said of the goods she bought from one moneylending company,

I do tell [the collector] sometimes ... I've seen it a lot cheaper in the shops but I've never got the cash to pay it really. They do put a good bit on.

This customer felt that she had little alternative but to pay,

I do think it's a lot on top. Like I said, £160 what he said was available at the moment. I'm sure it was £240 odd, you know, to pay back. It's a lot of interest again. And some people, like maybe even me this year, will have to have it because of the grandchildren really. You have to have it and you're paying all year then and before you know it it's Christmas again.

But although high rates of interest were seen as the biggest disadvantage of moneylending, customers had other complaints. When some companies gave people a loan they always took out the first payment for that loan at the time of handing over the money. For example, someone who borrowed £100 would have been given £100 but then would have immediately handed back £10 as the first repayment. So, in fact, the customer would only really receive £90. Some collectors and managers were unsure about the legality of this practice, but it was known to happen with a number of companies so the assumption was that it must be legal somehow. But even if it was legal, it was not considered just by many of the customers who knew about it and by some of the collectors from companies who did not have the same system. It was felt that if someone borrowed £100, they should at least be able to use that money before they started paying for it.

One of the larger companies said that, according to the contract between the company and customer, the first payment for any loan is due at the end of the calendar week, that is, the Saturday after the loan was made. As many loans are made on Thursdays and Fridays it was thought to be sensible for a collector to take the first payment at the time the loan was made rather than return one or two days later. The company further stated that the quoted APR reflected the fact that a first payment was removed. While it is reassuring that the stated APR takes into account the removal of the first payment, there is still the issue of the perceived fairness of the practice.

Another practice, which only some companies indulged in, was to take out a bank holiday payment when they gave someone a loan. For example, if Christmas was coming and someone wanted to borrow £100 six weeks before the holiday, the company would only give the borrower £90 and would not collect the payment which was due Christmas week. They said that this was because many customers missed their repayment at this time, but even so, their customers were receiving less than the money they had officially borrowed.

Insurance for sickness, accident or death was a bone of contention among some customers. Once again, companies had different practices when it came to insurance. With some companies, insurance was compulsory for all customers. Other companies gave people the option of having insurance and varied in the degree of encouragement they gave to customers to pay it. One manager was particularly scathing of insurance. He thought that it was an unnecessary extra expense which few customers benefited from. Some companies said that they provided free insurance either for death or sickness and death. But this would have to be paid for somehow and would therefore be reflected in the total charge for credit.

Some customers were very sceptical about the insurance which, in some cases, they were forced to pay. One woman had paid insurance and then was angry when it did not cover her husband for unemployment.

So there were clearly pros and cons of using a moneylender, which were succinctly summed up by one customer,

> There's not piles and piles of paperwork before you get an answer – and usually it's a refusal [from a mainstream lender]. The agent is very friendly. If for whatever reason you can't pay him on the Friday, he doesn't mind calling back on the Saturday. Minus wise there's the interest, but you can't do much about that.

KEY POINTS

- People use moneylenders for a combination of positive and negative reasons.

- When they first become customers, most people are on a low income but are not in dire financial straits. They choose to borrow from a moneylender because their access to mainstream credit is limited (with the exception of mail order).

- Even where other forms of credit are available, they are not always suitable. For example, bank and building society loans often involve large amounts and monthly repayments.

- Customers prefer to use a moneylender rather than go without or try, with difficulty, to save.

- Moneylending has several advantages for the low-income consumer compared with mainstream credit – small loans are available which can be repaid on a weekly basis to someone who calls for the repayments at a convenient time. And most companies do not levy any default charges if some repayments are missed.

- Most customers realise that they are paying a high price for credit but perhaps do not quite understand how much more expensive moneylending is compared with other forms of credit.

- As time goes by, some customers suffer a downturn in their financial circumstances. Their access to other forms of credit becomes even more limited and even less suitable. Their dependence on the moneylender grows.

5   The Borrowing and Lending Process

As we saw in chapter 3, new customers were taken on when they were in relatively strong financial situations. But these situations changed. The critics of moneylending argue that people become hooked to moneylenders so that even though they might be happy to borrow from them at first, it soon becomes difficult to break free. This chapter of the report explores the continuing relationship between moneylenders and their customers.

Staying a customer
The majority of customers (about two thirds) had used the moneylender 'more or less' ever since they had first borrowed from them. This period varied from about 7 months for the newest customer to 43 years for the longest-standing customer. The remaining thirs of customers had had one or more significant breaks from using the moneylender, usually when their income level changed. But there was no general pattern related to the direction of that income change.

For many people, as soon as one loan finished or was nearing an end, they would, almost automatically, take out another loan or buy some more goods. To understand this, we have to think back to how people made decisions about borrowing. It is generally assumed that people borrow money because they identify a need and then decide that borrowing the money is the best means of satisfying that need. This type of decision-making was relatively common when people first became customers – 17 of the 31 customers interviewed had become customers in this way. But after a while, many of them began to act differently. After the first few loans, they became a regular customer of the moneylender and knew that the moneylender would lend them, say, £200 once every 20 weeks. At the end of every 20 weeks or just before, they would borrow the £200 and then decide what to spend it on. So rather than identifying a need and then deciding to borrow, many people had got into a habit of borrowing from a moneylender.

To some extent, this habit is encouraged by the moneylenders themselves – as we shall see later in this section. But another reason for this habit, was the importance of regularity, security and control over money to people living on low incomes. For many people, borrowing from a moneylender had become a way of managing money rather than a source of credit. After a while the money paid out was not missed. This was either because it was a relatively small amount or because it was paid to the collector as soon as the family received their wages or benefit cheque. So people became accustomed to living on whatever was left after paying their moneylender every week.

This was the case whether people were using a moneylender to pay for consumer goods, to iron out the ups and downs in their income or to help pay for household bills. But those who borrowed to finance consumer goods usually had much higher chances of breaking the habit of borrowing from a moneylender than those who needed the money to pay for household bills.

Because of this constant renewal of loans, many people found it difficult to give details of their last loan. Some could not remember what it was for or when it was or how much they had borrowed. As one couple in their 40s explained,

> *It's hard to say, because, as I say, when one runs out then it's sort of renewed usually with another ... it's force of habit more than anything. You're actually paying this money out each month ... so you're always paying out the same amount constantly ... you usually end up finding something that needs paying or whatever.*

One couple, now in their 70's, had migrated Southwards to find work in the late 1930s. They had had three children and started using the company after the Second World War. The present collector's father had collected from them at first, then the son took over. They had used the company more or less ever since the 1950s. As soon as one loan had been repaid they would take out another. There was always something which was needed, children's clothes and household items at first. Now the money was used to repay bills such as the water rates and TV licence.

In some cases, customers borrowed the money and then were unable to identify a need. These people sometimes saved the money borrowed until something came up. They preferred to borrow the money and save it rather than break with their collector. The divorcee who borrowed to gain financial independence did not always use the money borrowed immediately. As she explained,

> *I don't go out and spend it recklessly. If there's nothing I want, I put it in the bank. It's more of a security thing, really. I pay all my bills through that.*

This practice of saving a loan was partly due to the desire among customers to keep open this source of credit. There was a fear that if they stopped using the moneylender they might not be able to get another loan in the future.

Although many customers got into a habit of borrowing from a moneylender, others did stop using them. Some of these may never use a moneylender again, but these would not have been covered in this study, since it only includes current customers. Others who took a break from moneylending did so because they had experienced a change in income which either enabled or forced them to stop using the moneylender.

One young woman had started using the company to buy consumer goods when she was still living at home with her parents. When she left home and got married, she stopped using the company as she had more money to buy the things she wanted. She returned to the company when her husband left her. He had previously borrowed £700 from her parents who now needed the money back. He was not prepared to pay them back, so she decided that her only option was to borrow the money. She borrowed the money and had to repay £12.60 a week for two years. The total repaid was therefore £1300 – an APR of about 100 per cent. She had to find this money out of the £70 a week she said she received in income support for herself and her three children.

Another woman had started using the moneylender's company in 1947. She had used them until she had been made redundant in the 1980s. When this happened she stopped using the company because she said that she could not afford to have them anymore. But a few years later, when still out of work, she was tempted to buy something from one of the vans which visited the area and she had been a customer again since then.

A couple had also stopped using the moneylender when one of them was made redundant and it looked unlikely that they would ever find another job. They thought that they ought to tighten their belts and *'don't have too much debt'*. But after a year or two they got into debt and borrowed £200 from their old collector to repay their poll tax arrears.

One couple had used their moneylender 'on and off', but then, when money got tighter they found that they were using him all the time,

> *Sometimes we've left it for quite a while and we've had a bill come in or we wanted to buy something quick or at Christmas or something. And it's on the phone to [the collector] ... but I've been having them sort of regularly, as one's finished I've been renewing it, for about the last year. The year before we sort of had them and then it would lapse and we'd finish it. But ... money's a bit tighter so you know we've needed the money for bills and we've not had it so we've been using [the collector] regularly.*

Some people did not get into a habit of borrowing or feel compelled to return to moneylending after a break. They only used the moneylender *'on and off'*. They were able to use credit from moneylenders when they wanted to and did not use it all of them time. One woman was quite relaxed about using the moneylender,

> *I've been with [the collector]] for a long time, I wouldn't give [the collector] up actually. I have been two years without ever going near him, but I have his phone number and if I rang him up tomorrow and said, '[Keith], I need you,' he's there, he is. And when I've finished they don't come back and hassle you.*

Another woman had first used the company in 1964 when her children were small and her husband was on relatively low wages. She had bought checks which she had used to buy furniture. She had used them on and off until her children were no longer at school and then took a break. She had recently begun borrowing money from the company, but only renewed her loan when there was something specific she wanted.

So the majority of people tended to get into a habit of borrowing from a moneylender. For many, it was a habit that they were happy with, or at least accepted as an inevitable way of life on a low income.

Continuing to borrow

Moneylenders, like all credit companies, are in business to encourage customers to borrow as much as they can afford to repay. This 'critical point' is not easy to find and may change as people's circumstances alter. To a certain extent moneylenders are sales reps and so we would expect them to try and sell their product as well as they can. But it is argued that moneylenders push people to borrow more than they really want to. And that some people are vulnerable to hard-sell tactics so that those who can least afford it may be encouraged to get into serious debt.

Encouraging people to borrow

For those companies that sold goods, collectors tended to turn up with brochures, catalogues or samples when the customer was getting towards the end of a loan. As one customer explained,

> *I had only a couple of pounds left [on a loan] and he was bringing in stuff all the time and I wasn't interested because I don't buy anything for the sake of buying ... I think I mentioned something about us getting a new stereo and there, lo and behold, the next week he had his brochures and then I thought, £200. Although we're paying the extra, it is a nice little system, the sound is great. And I thought, 'yeah! So he's got me into another thing.' But I wasn't going to buy anything. If I need something I buy it. If I don't, I don't.*

Another customer always succumbed to the temptation to buy when her collector brought samples of his goods with him,

> *You see if you're in your own home and he pulls up and he's got some nice things in the car, you're very, you know, tempted to buy and I do quite a lot. I mean at Christmas I buy a lot of the ladies' jumpers and the men's stuff for presents.*

A third customer knew that she could get goods cheaper through a catalogue but said that, '*he just talks me into having stuff.*'

One woman was aware that moneylenders had a reputation for being tough and aggressive. She knew that the reality was different and that the subtle tactics were much more successful. Her mother, who was also a customer of the same collector, turned up during the interview with her daughter and she joined in the discussion,

> *MOTHER: They encourage you all the time to be in debt with them, you know what I'm saying?*
> *DAUGHTER: Even though you've got arrears or whatever, they still encourage you to have the next loan.*
> *MOTHER: He'll say, 'do you need more decorating done?' or, 'don't you fancy a new carpet?' or something, you know, silly things. Of course, sucker, you fall into it.*

Through getting to know their customers and seeing their homes and children, collectors could suggest that they buy certain things. One of them summed up his persuasive abilities,

Oh he'd charm the pants off the queen he would!

But one of the things they liked about him was that he used charm and cheek rather than being overtly pushy,

He's very nice, there's a pleasant nature about him.

Another collector displayed the cheekiness mentioned by one of the managers when she managed to sell a hamper to a customer who ran her own hamper agency. As the customer explained,

She knew that I did the hampers and I kept saying I didn't need one because I do my own and she said, 'yes, but you haven't seen ours yet.' I mean she's laughing all the time she's saying it, like. And I had a look at the leaflet off her and I must admit this one was a good one so I cut down on what I ordered off my own and I had this one off her.

One of the collectors said that he never pushed people into borrowing. He would merely leave a catalogue with people. This was because,

The easiest thing in the world is to get something into a house but to get the payments afterwards, it's something completely different.

Those companies dealing mainly in cash loans had a harder time selling to their customers. They tended to do it by finding out what things the customer might want to buy and then suggesting that they take out a loan for it. The woman who went on holiday abroad every year had only thought to take out a loan for the first one because she had been talking to her agent about how she really wanted to go on holiday but couldn't afford it. It was the agent's suggestion that she borrowed the money.

But sometimes these tactics could backfire in the collector's face if they did not use sufficient subtlety. As one customer said of another collector she had used in the past,

She was a very abrupt woman and she used to come in here sometimes and she used to make really sarcastic remarks, 'Isn't it about time you decorated?' or 'Isn't it about time ...' you know. And that was another reason [why I stopped using that company].

The young woman who said that her collector could 'charm the pants off the queen' also spoke about a collector from the same company that had called on her when her usual collector was on holiday,

> *He was the nastiest man I have ever met in my entire life. He was rude, he'd got no manners.*

She said that if he had continued working on the round, she,

> *... wouldn't have anything else. I'd pay off what I owed and that's it, I'd finish. I wouldn't go back to it. Too nasty. Very abrupt.*

So the manner in which collectors dealt with their customers was crucial to their success. Many customers said that they liked their current collector precisely because they did not try to push anything on to them. As one said,

> *There have been times when I've finished and I haven't taken out another one straight away. She's never pressured me into it at all. So, you know, that makes you feel a lot easier.*

Another customer had a similar view,

> *He never pushes you, he's very good. When you're coming near the end of one, I generally say if I'm going to have another one ... he doesn't put you in over your head.*

Another customer was not very keen on one of her other collectors because she had tried to make her feel that she ought to take out another loan,

> *She kept on for quite some time before, when [my son's loan] was coming towards the end, kept asking if he was interested in having another and we kept saying 'no'. Then he finished it and the same went for me and when my husband came towards the end, it was the last one and we did actually have another one with her in my husband's name. But I turned round joking and I said to her, 'Are you happy now that you've had another one?' And she says, 'Well, not really, no, because you haven't had one'.*

This customer was no longer using that company.

As well as identifying potential needs of their customers, collectors used other tactics to try and increase sales. One collector in particular made a point of telling customers that they received a bonus when a customer took out a loan. Over the weeks and years, the collector 'conditioned' customers by praising them when they took out a loan. When one customer took out a loan in my presence, the collector remarked that the customer was 'doing them a good turn'. If people were thinking of taking out a loan, the collector would encourage them by saying that they had not arranged many loans that week and that they would not reach their target unless someone helped out by taking a loan. The collector tried to identify with their customers by saying that they needed the money and that the managers would not be happy if they did not meet the target. This was the most manipulative way of encouraging people to borrow. It used the friendly relationship built up with customers in order to increase business.

One customer admitted that she had taken out loans from a previous collector because she was,

> *soft-hearted. I liked to help her out ... I did it for custom for the girl.*

But collectors varied in the extent to which they tried to manipulate their customers. One customer compared two collectors that she had used,

> *[Pat] was very loud. I mean she was really nice, very nice. But she was a bit pushy, whereas [Lesley], if I say, 'no, thanks,' away goes the papers. With [Pat], it was, 'go on, go on, because you're helping me out,' and then that makes you feel guilty, you know. But with [Lesley], you know, she don't give a damn about her commission. If you don't want the stuff, then don't have it, you know, she is really good.*

Another way of encouraging business was to threaten, albeit in a subtle way, that if someone stopped using the company, they might not be able to use them again in the future. This played on all the fears of loss of security, mentioned above. One customer said that she always renewed loans with one of her moneylending companies, precisely because she did not want to risk the complete loss of this credit source. As she explained,

> *With [one of the companies] I've got down to where I'm only paying, say £10 a week and I've only got five or six weeks left to pay and [the collector] starts panicking, you know, 'you've got to have another loan,' you know. And she really panics because she thinks I'm going to finish with her, which I never do. I mean I get right down low and then I might want £500 for something, you know ... she just says, like, 'do you realise you've only got five or six weeks?' 'yes,' and then I*

> *might take out a loan for about £100 to keep it going until a time when I do want a large loan. Because their policy was – she says it doesn't really apply to me – but it always frightens me a bit: if you are a new customer and you went to [the company], you can't get a large loan right in the beginning, you have to build up to it. So once they get to know you, sort of thing, you can have a large loan. So I've never really finished with her completely because I think to myself, 'well perhaps I might want £500 and she'd say, 'well you have been finished for a while and perhaps you can't have it'', sort of thing. So I tend to keep it going.*

This quote illustrates the mutual dependence between the collector and the customer. The collector started panicking at the prospect of losing a good customer. The customer actually laughed about this and seemed to enjoy the power she had over the collector. But the collector had the last laugh because the customer would not risk the loss of her credit-worthiness by taking a break from the collector. It is unlikely that the customer would have lost her credit-rating if she had taken a break. The lone parent mentioned earlier who had taken out a £700 loan to repay her parents, had taken it out from the very same company. This was her first loan after a period of several years without using the company. While it is true that companies only lend small amounts to most new customers, they may be willing to take a risk if they have some previous knowledge about the customer. But, of course, some collectors do not want their customers to know this. They want to keep the customers as dependent on them as possible and so fuel any fears that the customer might have about losing access to an important source of credit.

Collectors deployed their most powerful persuasion techniques on their better-off customers. They saw little point in encouraging poorer customers to borrow if that meant great difficulties in collecting the repayments. So the most vulnerable customers, those who were poorest, were of the least interest to the moneylender and were put under the least pressure to borrow.

As well as encouraging people to buy new goods or take out new loans when their current repayments were finished, there was also some encouragement to people to renew their old loans before they were completely finished. Information from the companies suggests that the proportion of customers who renew before the end of the originally agreed term varies from 10 per cent of customers in one of the larger companies to 55 per cent in one of the smaller companies.

Renewals are one of the more contentious areas of moneylending. Critics argue that the customer is being charged interest on interest because part of the new loan is being used to pay off unearned interest on the old loan. But customers do have legal entitlements to rebates which are applied to the unearned interest on the old loan. The formula used – known as the 'Rule of 78' – gives an approximation of an actuarially correct rebate.

The statutory rebate system never gives people as much money back as they would intuitively expect. For example, if someone borrows £100 with £40 charges over a period of 20 weeks but repays all the money in 10 weeks, they might expect to have a rebate of half the charges – £20. But, as is the case with mortgages, at the start of a loan, more of each repayment will be interest than at the end. This means that the customer will receive less than half the charges if they settle half way through the loan.

There is a further complication to the statutory rebate system which is known as the '8 week deferral period'. Since there are some administrative costs involved with settling a loan earlier than scheduled, companies are allowed to defer the early settlement by 8 weeks. This means that the rebate for the customer who settles a 20 week loan 10 weeks early will be calculated as if they had settled only 2 weeks early. Using the example given in the previous paragraph, the customer would therefore get very much less than the £20 they might have expected.

Given the deferral period and the way interest charges are repaid at the beginning of a loan, customers generally receive little in the way of rebates. Moreover, customers with very short loans are often entitled to no rebate – on a 13 week loan, a customer will only be able to get a rebate if they settle 5 weeks after taking out the loan.

Some companies have more generous rebate systems than the statutory one.

While it may be the case that the existence of a rebate system means that customers are not, in theory, being charged interest on interest, the way the system works in practice means that the effective APRs on the new loan will be extremely high.

The industry argues that other types of credit – such as mortgages – are also subject to refinancing (renewals). They argue that moneylenders are not pushing customers into renewing loans but that they are merely responding to demand. In some cases, they may even try to stem that demand if they do not feel that the customer should renew early.

There was some evidence, however, of collectors who started encouraging customers to buy new goods before their old loans were finished. One customer succumbed to this tactic and only wanted to know how much more a week she would have to pay if she settled early. As she explained,

> [The collector] says, 'do you fancy anything? Bedclothes, hair-drier, anything like that?' I say, 'What you got?' when I know my bill's gone down and I'll say, 'How much does it cost me more a week if I pay for the one whatever I've had before that?' and [the collector will] say, 'well, it'll only cost you an extra quid or something like that.' So I don't mind that.

Although the customer did not mind 'an extra quid' a week, she was effectively paying dearly in terms of interest.

While on one of the observation rounds, the following interaction took place. A customer had two loans, one of which was virtually finished. The other was about half way through. The customer wished to finish off her first loan and take out a new one. The collector advised her to settle both loans and replace them with one new one. The collector presented it in such a way that if the customer did what she wanted to do she would pay much more each week than if she settled both loans. This was, of course, true, but the customer was not told about the implications in terms of the interest. After hearing the collector's advice, the woman still wanted to settle only one loan. But the collector was insistent that she was making a mistake and she eventually agreed with the collector's advice. After leaving the house, the collector was very pleased and said that it had been in the customer's best interests because she was paying less per week than she would have otherwise. But the collector was also very pleased because it meant that more money was collected – and so more commission received – than if the customer had succeeded in doing what she had originally wanted.

The following hypothetical example, based on the above case, illustrates renewals. A woman has two loans for £100 which are each spread over 20 weeks at £6.50 a week. So she is currently paying £13 a week overall. She has £13 left to pay on one loan and £65 left to pay on the other. She wants to take out another loan for £100 and pay off the smaller loan with the money. If she does this, she will have £87 in her hand and will have to pay £6.50 a week repayments for her new loan and £6.50 for her old loan (a total of £13). Her collector advises her to take out a loan for £150 and use it to settle both loans. She agrees. From this £150 she pays off the £13 and the £65 owed on both previous loans. This leaves her with £72 in her hand and she only has to pay £9.75 a week. Put in this way, it might seem that the collector's advice is right because the customer is paying less each week and has almost as much money in her hand. But she now has to pay for that money over the next 20 weeks. If she had done what she wanted, she would have finished paying for her second loan in 10 weeks and so would have had her total repayments reduced from £13 to £6.50 for the remaining 10 weeks.

Customers often said that the system of borrowing from moneylenders was easy to understand. In many ways it is, but the collectors often tried to make the system seem simple where there were complications. When the customer mentioned above was unsure about whether to renew or take out a further loan, the collector said that it was obvious that a renewal was better and did not explain the drawbacks.

Other collectors did not encourage people to renew early, but customers still did and it was a vital part of the business. One manager said,

> If people didn't settle and renew – and we don't encourage them, it's entirely their free choice – if they didn't I don't think we could survive on the rates we charge.

Although this manager said that his customers were not encouraged to settle early, the fact that they did so was not necessarily out of 'free choice'. Some people were so much in need of money and had no alternative source, that they had no choice but to ask if they could settle early and take out a new loan.

Some companies had guidelines about renewals but managers and collectors had a fair degree of flexibility in dealing with individual customers. One company generally allowed customers to renew a loan if they would get at least one third of the loan in their hand after paying their outstanding commitment. This meant that they could borrow £300, repay £200 of an existing loan, and only receive £100 in their hands. Another company specified that customers should only renew if they had paid off the principal amount.

Anecdotal evidence from trading standards officers suggests that some moneylending customers have renewed loans within a week of taking out the original loan. In such cases they are not always given a rebate. This type of renewal is extremely worrying.

Although collectors were good at encouraging business, they were not always keen to push their business as much as their managers wanted them to. One collector had left her previous company because she disliked the pressure put on her to increase sales. Another collector said,

> *Agents are ... told that they've got to do this and they've got to do that and, you know, 'we want more business, we want more business, you've got to do more business,' so what do you do? You tend to load the customers who are paying you well, don't you? And then you end up then, they go bad. I mean you can have customer paying you a fiver every week, never misses. But the minute you take them up to a tenner, it starts missing.*

This collector was aware that in searching for the 'critical point' where people were borrowing as much as they could afford to repay, there was a chance of overstretching people. The pressure to increase sales did lead to arrears,

> *Obviously every business ... has got to expand ... and we are encouraged to do more and more and more, but if I could do the job how I would like to do it where there was no, not pressure, but where you're not expected to do more each year, you wouldn't have hardly any bad debt at all because you'd keep people ... without knowing what they bring in, I know what people can afford ... it comes with experience.*

Another collector mentioned the persuasive tactics used by the manager to increase business,

> *There's no question of bullying or anything like that. In [my manager's] case, he just keeps stirring you to greater things, 'you've nearly done this,' and, 'you've nearly done that,' ... positive thinking, that's right, 'you achieve one percentage' and 'you do this just once more and you'll get this and get that', you know.*

It is interesting that the managers used the same methods to encourage their agents to sell as the agents used to encourage their customers to buy. The emphasis was on persuasion and subtlety rather than coercion.

Discouraging people from borrowing

Moneylenders were under pressure to encourage their customers to borrow. This was partly a self-induced pressure because it was related to how much money they earn. But pressure also emanated from their managers who were keen to increase company profits. Some collectors resisted these pressures more than others. One collector said that he hardly ever encouraged people to borrow more,

> *As soon as I get a new account, the first thing I tell them is, 'you are quite welcome, if you are a good customer and you pay this debt, to renew. Ask me for a renewal at the end of the loan, but I will not ask you if you pay me up and I never ever turn round and say, ' do you want another loan?'' It's got to be them to ask me and we give them the letter. We have the letters printed out and they just fill them in. And this is the law and that's how it should be.*

One of the collectors said that he was often pressurised by customers to renew a loan earlier than he thought was best for them. He was a sole trader and so decided to tell his customers that it was a CCA rule that he could not renew a loan before a certain time. For example, on a 14 week loan, he could only renew if they had paid back 10 weeks of repayments. He used the authority of the CCA because he wanted to distance himself from the decision. Customers would accept the decision if it was beyond his control. If it had been down to him (as it actually was) they would have pleaded with him more and might have been more upset at being turned down.

Some collectors said that they spent more time trying to discourage rather than encourage further borrowing. Some people wanted to borrow more even where they were not managing to repay their current loan within the initially agreed number of weeks. The collector tried to discourage them. In some cases, this was because they were concerned about the welfare of their customers. But in the majority of cases, it was because the collector knew that it was much easier to lend than it was to collect and so, if they lent money to people who could not really afford to repay it, they would not earn much commission from it. So the interests of the moneylender were, in some cases, the same as those of the customer.

As one manager said,

> *There's no money to be earned out of bad debt ... I think the outside world, outside the trade, always think we're pressing people to have loans and that's completely wrong. Nobody in our organisation puts*

*any pressure at all on anybody to either have a loan or anything else
... the pressure actually comes from the customer ... not from us trying
to force them into debt, that's the last thing in the world we would
want.*

Another manager explained,

*I never push anything on any customer at all because it's great to be able
to push things on to people, but it's no good if they can't pay for it*

But sometimes firms took a few gambles if their business was not
doing too well and they feared losing customers to rival companies.
As one manager explained,

*You have to be careful not to over-indebt people, but it's very difficult
because there are other firms going round as well.*

One collector said that if someone who was having difficulty
paying a current loan wanted another, he would show them their
payment book to explain why he thought they should either wait or
take out a smaller loan. He said that they would accept this but that it
was always difficult to refuse someone credit because it was a blow
to their pride.

Most people accepted this but one collector found some customers
less understanding. He said that one customer had been,

*... pestering me for ages. But they can't understand that I have to
answer to a boss back there ... people are oblivious to the fact that
they're doing anything wrong. [They think] it's alright to miss you –
'See you next week [John]', 'Sorry, we're going away, don't call for
three weeks, we're off on holiday,' to them there's nothing wrong with
it and alright, there isn't, but it's when they come and ask for me and
I have to say, 'look, I can't just give it to you.' .. you don't mind the
odd miss ... but when they should be paying you a five or £15 a week
and they're paying you £1 a week ... and then they're asking you for
more money – but they can't see that. They think it's my money and
they think, 'oh, you're bloody hopeless, you are! You give my mate
so-and-so. You give her anything she asks for! So-and-so asked for
£300, she got it!' ... That so-and-so must be paying regularly, she can
have it. But they don't understand that!*

Another collector remarked,

*I find that, most times I'm saying to people, 'you don't need that', 'do
you need it?' ... whereas probably the layman in the street ... they think*

*that you are knocking on the door saying, 'you've got to have that'
and getting people into debt.*

But there was a risk attached to discouraging people from
borrowing. If customers were refused a loan, they might go elsewhere
for it. And it could be even worse for the collector. For example, if
someone wanted to renew a loan early, or they already had one loan
going and they wanted another, and the collector refused, then the
customer might stop repaying their current commitments. So
collectors did not really want to have to say 'no' to their customers.
As one collector explained,

> *The last thing I want to say is 'no, you can't have it' because if I do
> that ... they really have always got the whip hand, because if they owe
> you 4-500 quid and you're saying no, the first thing some will say is,
> 'sod you!' or they use some stronger words than that, 'I'm not paying
> this ... so bugger off!' So you always have to keep on the right side of
> people.*

Even those who were keen to encourage some people to borrow
more, tried to discourage other customers. As customers got older
there was an increasing risk that they might die, uninsured. So
collectors tried their best to wean them off loans, even though they
were some of the more reliable payers. But this wasn't an easy thing
to do. As one collector said,

> *She pays me £10 a week and it's a nice clean little call. But she
> shouldn't be borrowing any more but it's very hard. How do you turn
> round to somebody that pays you and tell them, 'you can't have any
> more loans because you're getting too old', you know. It's very
> difficult.*

This collector had even talked to the woman's daughter who was
also a customer. He had asked her if she could try and reduce the
reliance of her mother on him.

Collectors varied in the amount of autonomy they had to grant or
refuse credit. In some companies, all loans had to be sanctioned by a
manager. In others, collectors would have discretion to grant or refuse
and would only discuss loans with managers when they were unsure
as to what to do. One way of refusing credit without damaging the
relationship between collector and customer was for the collectors to
distance themselves from the decision. Collectors would say that they

needed management approval before sanctioning a loan and could then explain that this approval was not forthcoming.

Turning someone down for a loan was often just a temporary measure. It usually meant that someone would have to wait a bit longer and reduce the amount owed or the number of loans before obtaining further credit. Customers were seldom entirely refused credit unless they paid very little every week and often missed paying even that. So even in refusing a particular loan at a particular time, there was a way for the customer to save face and continue to be a customer.

Making repayments
Ways of encouraging repayment
Most customers did not need encouragement to repay their loans. They felt a commitment to pay for what they had borrowed. They had entered an agreement with the moneylender and they felt obliged to fulfil their side of the bargain. This was not simply a business deal conducted on paper or over the telephone. It was one involving people face-to-face. If the collector was also someone friendly who had 'helped them out' in the past, the customer felt even more obliged to repay the loan. As one customer said,

> *We wouldn't like to miss him because he has been good with us, you know. We like to pay him up and that.*

But an added incentive was the knowledge that if they did not fulfil their side of the bargain, they might not be able to borrow from the same source again. This was particularly powerful where people had little alternative to using a moneylender for credit.

Some collectors tried to encourage people to pay by praising them when they did so and telling them about some of their customers who did not pay. This engendered sympathy for the collector and the customers felt that they did not want to let them down in that way. When people did miss payments, some of the collectors looked more hurt and dejected than angry. They had previously explained that they were paid by commission and so made it look as though they would be suffering from the loss of collection. They also made it known, on some occasions, that their manager would not be pleased with them. This was a clever tactic. Rather than say that the manager would not be pleased with the customer they tried to encourage sympathy and guilt from their customers by implying that they were getting them into trouble if they did not pay.

Levels of default

Although customers wanted to keep up with their weekly payments, two thirds (21 people), had some difficulties paying the total amount due every week. Ten of these missed payments from time to time, four were currently paying an agreed reduced rate every week and seven were paying the correct amount but were having trouble finding the money.

As we might expect, difficulties paying were related to the proportion of net income which went on payments. About half of all customers (14) were paying up to 10 per cent of their income in weekly repayments. Another 11 were paying between 10-20 per cent. The remaining 6 were paying more than 20 per cent. Generally, the higher the proportion, the more difficulty people had in paying. One pensioner couple were paying £65 a week out of their £120 a week income (that is, 54 per cent). They missed payments from time to time. At the other extreme, a working couple without dependants were only paying £10 a week out of their £300 net income (that is, 3 per cent). They did not have any difficulties finding the money. But proportion of income spent on repayments was only a general guide to difficulties. As we shall see, one of the lone parents was paying £30 a week from her £80 a week benefit and was having no difficulties finding the money because of the support of her extended family.

Difficulties with payment were also linked to how people used moneylenders. Those who used a moneylender to buy consumer goods were much less likely to have problems than those who borrowed to iron out ups and downs or to pay for bills and essentials. In the examples given above, the pensioners were using the moneylender to pay for bills whereas the lone parent was borrowing to buy consumer goods.

Of course, there was a link between these factors. Those who were borrowing to pay for bills and essentials were often on lower incomes than other groups and were repaying larger proportions of their income to the moneylender. Pensioners, in particular, were more likely to be borrowing to pay for bills and repaying large amounts of their income. Four of the nine pensioners missed weekly payments, one was paying a reduced amount, three were paying the full amount every week but having difficulties in doing so and only two were using the moneylender without any problems. Previous research shows that pensioners are very unlikely to get into debt (Berthoud and Kempson

1992) but missing the odd payment from a moneylender was not generally seen as default. It was accepted by moneylender and customer alike and no extra charges were added.

Unlike the pensioners just mentioned, older couples of working age who did not have dependants were generally more likely to use the moneylender to buy consumer goods and had a smaller proportion of their income taken up in weekly payments. None of these couples were missing payments or paying reduced amounts.

Those using the moneylender to iron out the ups and downs in their income did tend to miss payments when times were particularly hard.

So almost a third of customers interviewed missed weekly payments from time to time. Information from the companies about all their customers suggest that 20 per cent of customers missed a payment during any given week although one of the smaller companies put its figure at 50 per cent.

For some customers, missing a payment was a common phenomenon. As one remarked,

> *We are regular payers. But 'regular payers' on an estate like this means, 'they're lucky if they get it'!*

As mentioned, some of the pensioners found it particularly difficult to afford their repayments. One woman was 67 and had income of about £70 a week. She was repaying a total of £21 a week to the moneylender. This wasn't easy to find as she explained,

> *I can't pay too much, see, with the money what I'm paid, I've got to pay for all the electric light, gas bills, all that. I don't get nothing out of it, well I had a packet of fags today. That's all I've had and I have to buy meals, a little bit of meals, less meals every time.*

Another pensioner was in his 70s. He cared for his disabled wife who slept in a bed in the living-room because she was not able to get up and down stairs. He said that when he could not afford to make his weekly repayment *'I ask to be excused.'* His weekly payment was £5.

Where some people missed payments every now and then, four had negotiated a reduction in the weekly payment due. One couple had borrowed just over £300 which they were meant to be paying back at £10 a week. But the husband had lost his job and the collector agreed that they could pay back the loan at £5 a week until the original amount borrowed was cleared. This meant, in effect, that the interest was lowered.

One pensioner couple had been doing several part-time jobs to supplement their pensions. They had borrowed heavily from the moneylender and repaid £44 a week. But they had lost some of their jobs and so negotiated to reduce their repayments to £24 a week from their income of about £130. Collectors often said that they preferred to collect something every week rather than have people regularly miss payments. This was because once customers started missing payments the situation could escalate all too easily.

One man was not paying anything to the collector. He had borrowed £500 in 1991. A couple of months later he had an accident at work and was no longer able to do that job. He negotiated with the collector that he would not pay anything more until his compensation claim was settled. At that time he would repay the original loan, plus 50 per cent of the original loan as a charge for not having paid on time. After two years, the compensation claim had still not been settled and the moneylender had received no further payments. The collector called on the customer every now and then to see how he was and how the compensation claim was going.

Seven people were having difficulties repaying their loans but they did not miss payments or pay reduced amounts. They put a high priority on paying back their loan and cut back on other things or 'made sacrifices' in order to meet their commitments. One customer said that they paid up for fear of what might happen if they did not,

> We make sacrifices to pay it so that we don't go over the limit or they don't come and hassle us. We don't like being asked for money because you don't pay it off. We know some people are very nasty. [Our company] has never been nasty to me. So we generally pay up.

Once again, the spectre of the loanshark acts as a mechanism to police the behaviour of customers.

Others wanted to keep up payments because they liked the collector and wanted to keep open their access to this source of credit.

Not all customers had problems repaying their debts. Ten of the 31 customers had never had any difficulties paying back their collector. This was partly because they were some of the better-off customers and partly because they were careful to limit the amount they borrowed. Some only borrowed small amounts or only bought a hamper or hired their TV through the moneylending company.

An exception to this was the lone parent mentioned earlier. She was paying £30 a week out of her £80 income support. She had not borrowed the money in desperation to pay bills but to finance the purchase of a camcorder. She said that she had no difficulties paying the weekly amount and never missed. The main reason for her ability to manage in this way was that she had very close family ties. She lived with her parents most of the time even though she had her own council flat. The extended family pooled resources for food and bills so she seldom went short of anything and seemed quite happy with her lifestyle.

A more typical case of someone who did not have difficulties repaying a loan was a woman who only owed £3 a week to the moneylender. Her partner was in paid work and she was paying the loan back at £5 a week just to clear the debt quickly. Some people did pay their loans faster than the originally agreed rate. Whilst such people would be entitled to an early settlement rebate, that rebate would be calculated on the same basis as for someone who paid the contracted amount each week but then settled with a lump sum midway through the contract. In other words, customers who paid increased instalments were incurring a higher real rate of charge.

As mentioned earlier, all companies are required by law to pay rebates of charges to customers who settle early but the application of the rules can produce very small rebates.

But not everyone who should have been entitled to a rebate seemed to get one. One couple remembered how they borrowed about £700 over 2 years. They actually repaid the loan in one year, but received no rebate. If they had remembered correctly, the company must have acted outside the law.

Moneylenders' reactions to default

There is a general view that moneylenders start to get heavy-handed when people default on their payments. This view was not borne out by the findings from this research. In fact, the industry appears to accept the concept of controlled 'slow' repayment. Many customers fall behind on their payments and this is viewed as normal, and within limits, acceptable.

Collectors generally believed that the best way to recover payments was to keep on friendly terms with the customer. If a collector in any way upset a customer, the customer might decide never to open the door to them again. And if that customer had only borrowed a couple of hundred pounds, then the costs of going to court to recover any outstanding amount made such a course of action very unattractive to lenders. So even if the collector was upset and even angry with a customer, they tried their best not to let the customer see this.

Most collectors made a distinction between people who defaulted for 'genuine' reasons and those who defaulted for other reasons. Defaulters were divided into three categories.

Some were seen as 'unfortunate' debtors. These people had genuine reasons for default such as unemployment, sickness and divorce. Also, where people were living long-term on a low income, the collector would accept that every so often a large expense might knock the weekly payment down the customer's list of priorities. Collectors were not quite so happy about this type of debtor since they thought that customers should manage their money to avoid difficulties.

Others were considered to be 'feckless' debtors. These were people who did not apparently have the self-discipline to ensure payment every week. They put a higher priority on other things and felt little obligation to repay their debt according to the agreed terms.

As well as 'unfortunate' and 'feckless' debtors, there were some defaulters who were labelled professional debtors or 'borrower-sharks' – as collectors sometimes called them – who deliberately set out to borrow and not repay.

These three categories of debtors – unfortunate, feckless and professional – have been identified in previous sociological work about creditors' perceptions (Rock 1973).

Collectors thought that they were in an ideal position to be able to categorise defaulters. They saw their customers virtually every week and knew what kind of work situation they were in. Because of their local knowledge, they might even know other people who worked in the same firm. So they would know if a firm was making people redundant. They would also know about the state of customers' marriages so a separation was not always a shock. Even where customers did not divulge the details of their work or personal lives, the collector would form a view of whether the customer was generally honest and 'decent'. So if an emergency occurred one week, they would know whether to believe them or not.

Collectors also took some of the responsibility if people defaulted. After all, they had usually made the decision or had the largest say in whether to lend to that person. If the customer could never have afforded to repay a loan, then they should not have been given it in the first place. Of course if someone was dishonest from the start, the collector had less to blame themselves about, but it was often a blow to their professional pride when they thought they had 'been done' by a 'knocker'.

Collectors accepted missed payments here and there without saying too much. Some collectors would ask the customer why they had missed. Others would not even ask because they thought that if there was a genuine reason they might embarrass the customer and if there wasn't a genuine reason then there was no point hearing a lie. All collectors agreed that the best way to increase repayments was to keep on friendly terms with a customer. As one collector remarked,

> *If I lend anybody money I do my best to get that money, not by, you know, being horrible and nasty because that doesn't get you anywhere, but by being decent to people. And 99 times out of 100 you get your money back eventually.*

One collector believed that he had won a customer from a competitor precisely because he had been more understanding,

> *I had a competitor calling on them at the same time ... I think he put a bit of pressure on them ... and got a bit naughty when they wasn't paying properly one period and eventually they paid him up and subsequently transferred what they were borrowing from him to me.*

Most of the customers who had had difficulties repaying, said that their collector had generally been sympathetic. One customer had always paid regularly but her sister who had been a customer with the same collector, had once missed many payments,

> *At one time, my sister had a breakdown. She was in hospital and that and he was smashing, you know. He had to wait a while for his money. He got it, but he was really understanding about it.*

One customer missed payments occasionally. Although she disliked the collector knowing too much about her personal business, she did appreciate that this came in useful when she had difficulties finding the money,

> *He's ever so understanding really ... he knows a lot about everybody's family, I don't tell him ... he loves to know your business but I mean in some ways, I think he'd understand if I couldn't pay him one week but it don't happen often. It don't at the moment because I'm only*

giving him £3 a week. I think it's when it comes towards winter and you've got to pay your bills, gas and electric and all that.

Another was also appreciative of their collector's reaction, when they fell behind with their repayments,

With us, she's been fair, considerate and if there's a problem, like my uncle died. It's got to be three months ago now and I was up and down to London like a yo-yo. And I owed her a fortune and she never once said, you know. She knew, death in the family. She knew there was a reason why I hadn't paid ... it was a genuine excuse.

One collector explained how he negotiated reduced payments with his customers,

We just say, 'What can you afford to pay? and we will accept what you can afford' ... we find that a lot of accounts do come down gradually. If they were supposed to be paying £10 a week and we're getting £1 or £2 a week obviously it's going to take a long time but it comes down to – we will accept what they offer – basically.

He continued,

You can't get blood out of a stone. The most successful way of doing it is to have a chat. Because people feel embarrassed sometimes and don't want to approach you because they can't pay. So you've got to break down that barrier and just have a chat with them without being threatening.

One customer had reduced her payments from £20 a week to £10 a week when her partner lost his job. Her perspective on these negotiations was as follows;

He came and we talked about it and said there would be no problem, the company are good providing you pay them something. It's better than not paying anything and they would see that. In fact they did send us a letter, didn't they and it was really nice, that under the circumstances they would reduce ... we were really pleased.

Slow payers were a particular blow to business in times of inflation. Periods of high inflation such as the mid 1970s caused great difficulties to some companies who saw the value of repayments fall.

But not all cases were 'genuine' ones. One collector prided himself on his ability to spot the difference,

I've heard all the excuses for not paying. They think they're fooling me when they say they can't pay because so-and-so. I know when

people are genuine. You don't do something for over 25 years and not know when people are trying to pull the wool over your eyes. But they think they are ... I've heard all the excuses why they can't pay: they've lost their purse, the social have sent for the books back and they've had to lend the money to the sister, you know. You've heard it all and you know when people are telling you lies.

Another collector felt that his small company was vulnerable and exploited by some people who knew how to use the system. As he said,

We try to operate with a human face and some people sense that and they use us.

He gave an example of one case where he had been caught out,

Mum had borrowed a lot of money, between £1-2,000 on the promise of an insurance coming through and she paid. Daughter then perhaps a year or two later came in and she had an accident compensation coming through and borrowed between £1-2,000. Well, the mother had done it, so we thought, that's fine with the daughter ... the cheque had now arrived so next time we were due, we went round and she'd gone to [the Far East] with the money ... we lost £2,000 and that was a bitter blow ... once she'd blown that money, how are you going to get it back?

Another collector gave her own example of a professional debtor. A woman had bought a carpet from the company and borrowed a total of £300. The collector struggled to get the repayments for this carpet even though she could see no reason why the customer might have difficulty repaying. In the end, it took five years to collect the £300, which averaged out at about £1 a week. The collector was determined never to lend to that customer again and informed her managers about who she was and where she lived. But some time later a canvasser working in the area had sold the woman another item. The collector was furious and even though it was a smaller amount than before she dreaded the prospect of having to collect it.

These bad cases tended to stick in collectors' minds. As well as the loss of money, they were also a blow to their pride as they felt they had been conned. Because of their importance in business and personal terms, the one-off worst case tended to dominate a lot of the collector's thoughts and behaviour. Just as the spectre of the loanshark affected customers, the spectre of the borrower shark affected the lenders.

Many collectors felt angry when customers that they thought could afford to pay, did not. But they all agreed that there was no point showing that anger in any way. As one said,

I have to walk away from anybody's door knowing that I can go back next week and knock the door and they'll open it to me. The last thing I want to do is walk away with bad feelings and them thinking, 'well, sod you! I'm not going to open the door when he comes next week.' We've still got to collect our money ... and that's one of the annoying parts of the job is to walk away from somebody's door with them thinking they've pulled the wool over your eyes and you know they haven't.

Another collector had a similar view,

Occasionally you do have to put your foot down and say, 'look, we gave you this loan in good trust. You haven't kept up the payments. What is going on? And do you think it's right, yourself?' ... but it's no use exploding on doorsteps. The door will be shut and you've lost contact. You have to bear a lot of it. You've got to keep the contact open, you see. You might feel like screaming and shouting but you can't. You let off steam in the car.

Collectors often felt impotent when people did not pay. Most customers were sent letters from the company if they missed a few payments. The larger companies had a number of letters ranging in degrees of firmness about the default. The mildest letter was sent out first and then might be followed by a more strongly worded missive if there was no change in behaviour following the first. Some of the smaller companies did not have set letters and rarely sent such communications.

In some cases, the manager might visit the customer personally. This might occur after a letter had been sent or instead of a letter. A strange new face at the door, usually a male one, would sometimes encourage people to pay better.

But these methods were not always successful at restoring repayments. Or payments might be regular for a while and then drop off again. One collector commented,

If all my customers decide not to pay me, what can I do? I can't take a shotgun to their doors, can I? If you fall out with them, they don't pay. And the company will threaten, well not threaten them but send them letters, but they never carry it forward. That's why I don't like giving letters to customers.

Default charges were very rarely levied, except in cases where the customer expected to receive an insurance claim and the collector would agree to wait for their money so long as they would receive an extra amount. One customer had been warned that they might have to pay an extra charge, but there were no hard and fast rules about these charges. Indeed, they seemed to be the exception rather than the rule. So in a sense, the customers who were paying the full amount every week were subsidising those who missed payments or reduced amounts. Of course, this happens in many companies and some form of redistribution may be welcomed but all moneylender customers came from low-income groups and if some people were not paying because they were dishonest, it seems unfair to expect honest customers to pay extra.

Because of the small amounts of money involved, it was seldom thought worthwhile to take people to court if they did not pay the money they owed. The only way of recovering it was to keep knocking on the door.

Sometimes large amounts of money were lost through one customer and so pursuing this through the courts might have been worthwhile. But the owner-collector who had lost £2,000 when a customer spent it on a holiday in the Far East had not pursued the debt in the courts. As he explained,

> We have taken people to court, but we find that we're throwing good money after bad money to tell you the truth. We spend more money on solicitors to be honest. Some traders are very good and they take them to court themselves and have got the time to do it. I haven't got the time to do that.

Other collectors believed that customers would often lie to the courts and 'welfare advisers' such as Citizen Advice Bureau workers. For example, the collectors would know that some people had jobs 'on the side'. Income from these would not be declared and so it would appear that the person could not afford to repay very much.

One collector said that he had been 'taken on' by a 'professional' and thought there was little point going to court,

> I knew if I took her to court and had a bit of a battle I'd probably get a few quid a week and then what would happen, after a few weeks she'd stop. I'd then have to issue another summons and so it would go on and it's a pain then. It's a waste of time, not worth the effort

*and I had to write it off. And when you're a small man like me that's
a lot of money to write off.*

The main sanction against persistent default was therefore the
knowledge that non-payment would reduce credit-worthiness. And
indeed, this was often a powerful threat for people who had little or
no alternative source of credit.

So moneylenders did not become aggressive when people
defaulted. Indeed they were often fairly relaxed about default and
continued to lend money to customers who were already having
difficulties repaying their weekly instalments. Moneylenders argue
that as long as default is kept at a manageable or controlled level,
customers should retain access to credit. But what might seem a
manageable level of default to a moneylender may actually be a
weekly struggle for the customer to find the repayment.

Ending the relationship

All the interviews and observation work took place with existing
customers. No ex-customers were included but as we saw earlier, nine
people had had significant breaks from being a customer. These people
stopped using the moneylender either when their situations improved
and they felt they no longer needed credit from the moneylender or
when their situations got worse and they thought they could no longer
afford such credit. There were also some people who had stopped
using particular collectors because they were considered too pushy

The vast majority of customers could not foresee a time when they
would be without their moneylender.

About half of all customers were happy with the moneylender and,
although they would have preferred a lower interest rate, they were
prepared to pay for the service provided. Most of these were using the
moneylender to buy consumer goods. Some people said that they were
happy to continue using the moneylender and could see no immediate
reason to stop. But they said that they might take a break or stop using
if they wanted to. They did not feel trapped into using the
moneylender.

About a third of the customers, however, needed the moneylender
so much that the thought of not being able to use the service left them
very concerned. Eleven customers were in this situation, including the
divorcee in her early seventies. They did not want to end their use of

a moneylender because they needed it so much. Most of these were borrowing to repay bills and essentials.

Although most customers accepted that they would always use moneylending, many would have preferred to have been in a position where they did not need to use a moneylender or where they had more choice about using such a service.

Three customers could foresee a future without moneylending. One said that, while she accepted that she had to use the moneylender now, she would stop doing so when all of her six children were older,

> *Once they're all off my hands or madam here is old enough to start saving for her own things, whatever she wants, then, yeah, I would never have debt. This is what we've always said to these, 'always pay your own way because once you get into that, once they get their hooks into you ...' and it's so easy to go back to them again and I'd rather not them not live that way.*

This woman said that she definitely classed her use of a moneylender as debt rather than credit,

> *So does my husband, you know, he don't like it. He don't like it at all. But as he said, without it, some people couldn't survive and they couldn't. Because the wages are pathetic. You don't get enough money to live on now, so where else would you get the stuff from if you needed it? It's very hard.*

This woman certainly saw moneylending as a necessary evil. She disliked using moneylenders and hoped that she would soon be able to stop using them. But she felt that, at the moment, she had little choice.

Another two customers thought that their use of a moneylender was temporary. One had bought a duvet set from a canvasser and did not intend to buy anything else but then was encouraged to buy a CD. She did not expect to buy anything else but was happy to carry on if there was something she wanted and the price and quality of the goods was acceptable. Another woman had borrowed money to repay a debt to her parents. She had not expected to use a moneylender again once this debt had been repaid, but she had then taken out another loan to buy a computer game for her son as a Christmas present.

One man was not currently using a moneylender. His payments had been suspended while he waited for an insurance claim. He did not expect to use a moneylender again until after the claim was settled and he found himself another job.

Since there were no ex-customers in the study, it is interesting to see what other research can tell us about how and why people stop using moneylenders. PSI's in-depth study of 74 low-income families included 12 ex-customers of moneylenders (Kempson et al 1994). Most of these had stopped using a moneylender because of the high interest and difficulties with weekly repayments. As one explained,

> *We had a bedspread. I think it was £23 ... and when she came the following week, she writ the card down. It had gone up to about £29. I said to her, 'What you done that for?' She said, 'Well we have to put that down, it's for the APR and all this, you know, for coming back and forward. And I'd already received the goods, you see, and I'd signed for it and everything so there was no backing down. And I said I'd never do it again.*

This woman now bought goods from a mail order catalogue as did many of the others who no longer used a moneylender. Many preferred using a catalogue because of the lower total cost and the higher quality of goods.

Expensive and low quality of goods was a complaint of another ex-customer,

> *We'd never do that again. We paid over the odds ... and the sheets didn't last as long as the ones we'd already bought cheaper.*

As well as general criticisms of moneylending, some people had particularly bad experiences. One woman said that when she missed a couple of payments, the company started to 'get heavy'. She did not explain exactly what she meant by this. Another customer said that her agent had not been passing on her payments to the company and so she did not use moneylending any more.

Not all ex-customers were set against ever using moneylending again. One said that she did use moneylenders occasionally and would do so again but did not need to at the moment. Another wanted to use a moneylender again but had been turned down. She had previously used a moneylender when her mother had been alive. After a long break from using any moneylender she had tried to get a loan from a different company and was turned down. She thinks this was because she had a county court judgement against her for gas arrears. She was a lone parent with two children and her 82 year-old father lived with them.

For some customers, their relationship with moneylending lasts *'till death us do part'*. Although moneylenders tried to wean older people off their loans, this was difficult as they were often the people who depended on it most and were most frightened about having this 'lifeline' taken away. If someone had been a good customer for many years and needed it, it would be difficult for a collector to refuse credit. So collectors tried, in subtle ways, to reduce the amount these people borrowed. For example if an elderly customer asked to renew a loan they would advise them to wait a bit longer, then a bit longer. And when they did renew, the moneylender would ask them if they wanted to borrow a little bit less this time, saying that this would give them more money in their pocket. In some ways, the collector was putting forward all the arguments against moneylending.

KEY POINTS

- Some people do get into a habit of borrowing from a moneylender and take out a loan as soon as, or before, they reach the end of their current loan.

- Moneylenders generally use a combination of charm and cheek to encourage borrowing. Customers tend to stop using moneylenders they consider to be pushy.

- Many customers have difficulties repaying their loans. Contrary to their image, moneylenders do not become aggressive when people default. Indeed they seem to be fairly relaxed about missed payments and continue to lend to people who do not repay loans on time.

- The main sanction against persistent default is loss of credit-worthiness in the future. This is often a powerful sanction against those who have no alternative source of credit available to them.

---

6   The Nature of the Relationship

The relationship between the borrower and lender that develops through weekly doorstep collection is obviously central to any assessment of moneylending and forms the main part of this book.

The core of this relationship is the mutual dependence and mutual trust between the moneylender and the borrower. As Braudel states,

> *Credit is the exchange of two deferred promises: I will do something for you, you will pay me later. (Braudel 1973)*

The elements of trust, obligation and mutual dependence on the part of both lender and borrower are central to all credit transactions. The lender would not be in business without the borrower and the borrower would not be able to borrow money without the lender. But the amount of trust, obligation and dependence will vary between different individuals and within different relationships at different times. In some circumstances, the lender will be very dependent on the borrower. For example, they may have just lent a large sum of money and they are dependent on the borrower to repay it. Or a relatively affluent and good customer who borrows large sums and repays them quickly may be thinking of going elsewhere for credit. In other circumstances, the borrower will be very dependent on the lender. For example, they may want to borrow a large sum of money and they may have very few alternative sources of credit. Of course, the lender is usually lending to a large number of customers at one time so their dependence on any one is probably not too great. But if their business is just about breaking even, then they are particularly dependent on keeping some of the better customers. And borrowers may have other moneylending companies and alternative sources of credit so they are not necessarily solely dependent on the one moneylender.

Although trust, obligation and mutual dependence are features of all credit transactions, they are particularly important with moneylending through the face-to-face contact between lender and borrower. Such contact was once a feature of many credit transactions, for example middle-class people would see their bank manager in person to arrange an overdraft. Nowadays, mainstream lenders are more likely to use impersonal methods of credit assessment through use of an application form to collect factual details. 'Relationship banking' is on the decline and new services such as *First Direct* provide banking entirely over the telephone without any face-to-face contact.

All relationships operate on a number of levels and three aspects of the relationship between moneylenders and their customers are especially interesting. At a *personal level*, relationships varied in their level of formality. There were also variations in the *power balance* – that is, the degree to which the collector or customer controlled the relationship. Finally, the *underlying nature* of the relationship varied in the degree to which it was exploitative or supportive. These three aspects were linked but one did not determine the other. Each of these aspects had a continuum, as shown in the diagram below:

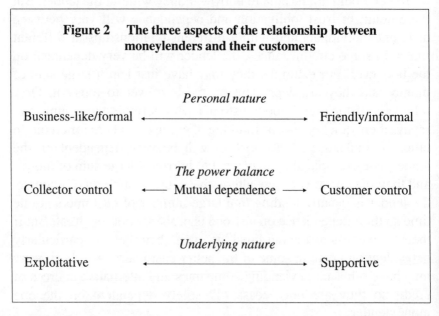

Figure 2   The three aspects of the relationship between moneylenders and their customers

Personal nature

Business-like/formal ⟵──────────────⟶ Friendly/informal

The power balance

Collector control ⟵── Mutual dependence ──⟶ Customer control

Underlying nature

Exploitative ⟵──────────────⟶ Supportive

The remaining parts of this chapter examine the three levels of the relationship.

The personal nature of the relationship

The personal nature of the relationship varied from the very formal relationship – where there was little personal interaction, to the very friendly – where the personal aspect was paramount.

Customers who did not have a personal relationship with a collector

Some customers had little or no direct personal relationship with their collector. Week on week, they did not even see the collector. These customers fell into one of two groups: those who were never at home, or at least never answered the door and those who handled all their transactions with the collector through a third party.

The collectors were not very sympathetic to the very small number of customers who rarely, if ever, answered the door to them. They emphasised that if people were having difficulties in paying, all they had to do was explain this and some arrangements could be made. The implication was always that if people were not willing to open their door, then they must be trying to avoid payment.

Collectors left notes through the door and sent letters to these customers, encouraging them to get in touch. Some were recent customers who had been taken on by canvassers, so the collector might never have seen or met them. But the collectors still visited the house every week, often at different times, to see if they could catch the customer in. They often viewed their relationship with these customers as a kind of battle. They had assumed that the customer was trying to avoid payment and they were determined not to let the customer 'win'.

These customers were not seen during the observation work and could not be interviewed as part of this study. So it is difficult to give their side of the story. Perhaps some of them were trying to avoid contact because they did not want to pay. Some might have been away from home for long periods of time. Some might be avoiding contact because they could not afford to pay.

The other group of customers who rarely saw the collector were people who gave their money to another member of the family who dealt with the collector on their behalf. It was most common for a woman to manage the payment for herself, her partner, her adult children and perhaps even her own mother. This arrangement was common where all adults living in the same family home borrowed from the same company. But on occasions it was set up by relatives who did not live in the same household. For example, one of the pensioners dealt with her nephew's account with the collector. His visit to her to deliver his weekly payments was one of the few times she ever saw a relative.

So there might be several customers in a family, and each could have more than one loan at the same time. This meant that moneylenders could sometimes collect over £100 in one house from such multiple accounts. This arrangement was very convenient for the moneylender. Rather than having to find convenient times for each customer or travel to each of the customer's houses, 'mum' would collect all the payments. Sometimes 'mum' would 'police' the other customers by pressurising them to pay the full amount every week. And sometimes she would also make up the difference if one of the family did not have enough money that week. The collector would not always see the other customers, but 'mum' would say how they all were. When the other family members wanted another loan they would make a point of being around when the collector called and this might be one of the few times when the collector saw that customer face-to-face.

There were also a very few people who used the moneylender but did not want their partner or other members of their family to know about it. They asked friends, other relations or neighbours to deal with the moneylender on their behalf. So, again, they had little or no direct personal contact with the moneylender.

None of these customers were interviewed and so it is not possible to say what they thought about their collector or the service they received.

How the customers felt about their collectors

The customers who were interviewed were generally happy with the collector they had. Of course, it should once again be remembered that these were all current customers. The collectors were seen as friendly and sociable but these qualities were usually linked to the business aspects of their work. Customers felt *grateful* for being lent money. A male customer who had used the same family firm for over 40 years said,

> He's been a good friend to me, moneywise. He helps out ... we understand each other.

Many customers appreciated the financial *'help'* they were given. Many said that their collector was *'very obliging'*. They were rarely turned down for a loan which saved their pride. So the boundary between the social and the business aspects of the relationship was extremely vague. Some people felt that their collectors had been *'kind'* to them when they had lent them money,

> *I like [John]. He's a very, very nice chap, very obliging. They're very good to us. They've all been very kind to us.*

But the same customer had a similar view of their relationship with the bank manager,

> *We hadn't got enough money [to bury a close relative] so we went to the bank manager and told him what we wanted it for and he kindly let us have it.*

Of course, 'kindness' may not have come into the decision to lend them money. Credit granting, particularly among mid- or up-market lenders, is generally based on objective criteria. But, on the margins, moneylenders do have discretion and can be swayed by personal feelings either to grant or refuse.

Several customers said that their collector was *'nice'*. When asked what they meant by this, they tended to reply in terms of the business aspects of their relationship rather than the personality traits of the collectors. For example, one customer commented that,

> *I've found he's very nice. He's a very nice man. He's very good ... I mean, if we need a loan and it's not a Friday, we can always phone his house and say, 'look, can we have a loan for Friday?' And if everything's alright we can have it for Friday ... he's just a friendly person I find, someone you can take to really.*

Another said,

> *He really is a nice person, you know? ... I mean when I come to be expecting with the first little one, he helped us out with vouchers for Argos for a pram because they were the cheapest place and it was Christmas time so we were a bit stuck. We'd just got married ... he's easy-going, pleasant, you know, nice personality and that and you won't feel like you're begging off him.*

A pensioner appreciated the fact that her collector tried to limit the amount she borrowed,

> *He's so kind and so caring. But he's firm. He thinks, well, if you don't really need it, he'll tell you. I can always rely on him. He's not pressing you to take out more than you can afford.*

Underlying the views of many customers was a low expectation of what a moneylender might be like. When asked what they thought about their collector, the first reaction from some customers was a negative positive,

I never got nasty calls.

Had no trouble.

I've never had any trouble with them.

It is almost as though these customers had been expecting 'trouble' or 'nasty calls'.

It could be argued, however, that the eight collectors involved in this study were atypical of all collectors. We have no reason to suppose that this is the case due to the way the sample was selected (see methodological appendix). But all customers interviewed were asked about the different companies and collectors that they had experience of. This enabled us to judge whether the agents involved in the study were typical. In most cases, very similar relationships emerged. For example, one customer talked fondly of a previous collector,

There was one chap, I'll never forget him ... and he'd sit and he'd say, 'come on then, let's have a cup of tea'. A lovely chap he was and he thought the world of [our daughter] ... and when he got up to go he used to put up three sixpences and say, 'give them to the nippers'. I never forgot him.

One woman customer still kept in touch with a woman who used to work as her collector,

She still comes round to see me, now. We got really friendly ... She had twins a year ago and she even brought the twins round to see us and things like that.

Another customer reckoned that he had *'struck lucky'* as far as his callers were concerned. One of them was *'as good as gold, that girl'*.

One woman had various collectors in the past. She preferred some to others,

[Larry] was one of those chaps that makes the hair on the back of your neck stand up, you know. Even though I continued to buy, he wouldn't have been encouraged to stay in the house long. I mean, I don't believe in keeping people at the door, but I wouldn't have made him feel so welcome as I do [John] ... the poor bloke's dead now, probably didn't mean any harm, but it's just that some people have

that effect on you ... [Peter] was nice, younger, nice bloke. Sort of quiet but nice as well, you know. You felt you could trust him. I could never trust that one that made the hairs stand up on the back of my neck. I never trusted him, always checked my cards, always made sure he put down what I paid ... but all the others I felt completely at ease with ... [Peter] was really nice, talked a lot about his family.

There were a few callers that people did not like because they were pushy. By and large, they soon stopped using them in preference to more pleasant and less pushy callers. This seems to be confirmed by other research which shows that most people who are unhappy with their collectors generally stop using them (Kempson et al 1994). But if a customer really needed the loan, they might accept, more or less, whoever was sent to collect the repayments. As one customer said,

He's a nice bloke, but I mean if it's helping me out, I don't mind who comes to the door.

How the collectors felt about their customers

The chapter of this report on *The moneylenders* gave some details of how collectors felt about their customers. The collectors said that they liked '90 per cent' of their customers. The remaining 10 per cent were made up of different types, such as those who had no intention of paying and those that they found to be personally unpleasant. For example, on one of the observation rounds, as the collector pulled up in her car, she explained that she was always 'greeted' by the next customer with the question, *'What the fucking hell do you want?'*. She explained that this was said in a half joking-half serious manner but she did not find it particularly pleasant. True to form, the customer came out to see the collector and gave his usual greeting at the top of his voice in the middle of the street. This was rather an extreme case. Some other customers were just irritating to the collector so that visiting them was not particularly enjoyable.

Although the collectors liked most of their customers, these feelings differed slightly for each collector. The 'one of us' collectors, who were generally women agents, saw things from their customers' point of view. The 'entrepreneurs' also had good relationships with most of their customers but were sometimes judgemental. The 'paternalists' were more detached from their customers but this detachment was often based on a mutual respect and paternalism.

The location of business and topics of conversation

It is interesting to see what customers and collectors said and thought about each other. But the observation work also provided another perspective. It showed that the nature of the relationship was reflected in the location of business and the topics of conversation between collector and customer.

Some customers saw their collector regularly each week, but only briefly. In these cases, the formal, business aspect of the relationship was paramount. The collector would knock on the door and the customer would open it with their book and money in hand. They would ask each other how they were and there would be some general chit-chat, for example about the weather. During this time the money and book would be handed over, the book filled in and returned.

These 'doorstep customers' particularly suited the part-time women agents who visited a large number of customers in a short amount of time. They did not have much time to talk with their customers. This type of encounter was also particularly common if the customer only paid a small amount of money every week. In a sense, they had only 'earned' a small amount of the collector's time. There were also some customers that the collector did not want to get too close to. These were some of the poorest customers living in accommodation which often smelt unpleasant. Collectors were relieved not to be asked in or resisted an invitation by saying that they did not have time to stop.

Some collectors disliked dealing with customers on the doorstep because of the dangers of being observed with cash by possible attackers. Rain and cold weather also made the location inhospitable at times and it was difficult to build up a good relationship while standing at the doorstep. So sometimes collectors would tactfully try to gain entry into their customers' homes.

But business on the doorstep suited some customers because it meant that they would not be disturbed for very long and could keep their personal life separate from their business dealings.

There was a compromise area which allowed customers to maintain their private space and at the same time allowed collectors to avoid the possible dangers of doing business in public space. This was the hallway. The collector would step into the hall and push the front door to, but not quite shut. The hallway often had the advantage of providing stairs for the collector to sit on. This made it easier to fill in their books. It also served as a way of breaking the formality of doing business in the hall. Female collectors, in particular, used the stairs.

Some customers seemed to prefer the hallway because it prevented 'nosy' neighbours from seeing too much of their business. And it also prevented the collector from seeing too much of their personal life.

Sometimes, however, the collector would gain access to some of the more private areas of the house. This was particularly common with the longer-standing older customers or with customers whose children were at school. Conversation with 'living-room customers' was generally about the extended family, whom the collector often knew. The social aspect of the relationship was important. Indeed, collectors sometimes found it difficult to get away from the armchairs of their older customers, who seemed most pleased to have their company. Although the collectors were quite happy to talk for a while, the pressure of getting on with business was often at the back of their minds. Some older people were 'good' customers, in that they paid a large amount every week and so the time spent with them was not begrudged. But some of the poorer customers borrowed only small amounts. Some of these customers had developed tactics for prolonging the stay of their collector. One held firmly onto her money and her book while she talked to the collector. She would not hand it over until she felt she had had 'her money's worth' of attention and time. The collector accepted that this was all part of the deal, but it did irritate her.

One woman in her 40s particularly appreciated the company of her collector,

> *With me not going out much ... both my husband and son are at work and I'm only on my own here. It breaks the day up for me just when [Lesley] comes because it's somebody to have a chat to, you know. If I've not seen anybody ... I get on well with [Lesley].*

The most informal and friendly calls were with the 'kitchen customers'. Busy mothers at tea-time would invite the collector into the kitchen or kitchen-diner. Tea-time – around 4pm – was a good time to find mothers with young children at home as they would often have just picked up their children from school. The kitchen was a very informal area which female collectors seemed able to make themselves particularly at home in. Conversation tended to revolve around the children. The collectors were often very good at communicating with children. They seemed interested in what they had been doing that day at school and so kept them occupied while the customer went to find her payment book and money. The lives of these 'kitchen customers' seemed very busy. Various adults and children seemed to be popping in and out all the time, there was food being prepared, the TV on, children playing on the floor, dogs and cats making their presence felt. Collectors had much to talk about with these customers and genuinely seemed to enjoy chatting. The female collectors were, or had been, in similar family situations themselves and so there was a great deal of shared experience, especially if these collectors came from the 'one of us' category.

The location of business was a guide to the nature of the relationship but the two were not always the same. Generally, 'kitchen customers' and 'living-room customers' had closer relationships with their collectors than 'doorstep customers' or 'hallway customers' but part-time women agents did have very close personal relationships with women customers that they only dealt with on the doorstep.

It is difficult to give details on how many customers came within each of these categories since the importance of the location of business was not identified before the observation work and so data was not collected during that time. And there was variation between collectors, with part-time agents having more 'doorstep customers' than full-time collectors and women collectors having more 'kitchen customers' than men. But, to give a very rough idea, out of 100 customers it is likely that 10 will not be at home or will not open the door on any particular round, 15 will not see the collector because a relative pays for them, 20 will be 'doorstep customers', 15 will be 'hallway customers', 15 will be 'living-room customers' and 15 will be 'kitchen customers'.

Factors which affect the nature of the personal relationship

Three factors affected the nature of the personal relationship between collectors and customers: the socio-economic characteristics of the collector, the socio-economic characteristics of the customer and the length of time that the customer had known the collector. This analysis must be somewhat tentative since only eight collectors were interviewed and observed.

In general, women collectors had more informal and friendly relationships with their customers than their male counterparts. This was the case even though, as part-time workers, they normally spent less time with their customers than did the men, who all worked full-time.

Women collectors were very relaxed with their customers and even in the space of a minute or two could find out the latest news on someone's marriage troubles or illness. Common topics of conversation included personal relationships, children, health and work situations. The success of the women in establishing relationships with their customers emanated from their willingness to divulge details about themselves and their families. This reciprocity was fundamental to a growth in friendship and trust between the collector and customer which was also very important to the business aspect of the relationship.

One customer compared her male collector, who always came in for a cup of tea, with a female collector from another company, who never had time for a drink. But the female collector and customer knew each other's families and so they had little difficulty relating to each other on a fairly deep level even in a short space of time,

> She's normally in too much of a hurry ... hers is just more like a part-time job for her, whereas [John] it's his living. She just calls on an evening ... I mean she comes in and I know all her family and she knows all my family and that, you know because we lived quite close.

The ability of women agents to build close relationships with their customers was mainly due to gender. Women seemed to be better generally at close personal interaction than men. There was some difference, however, between women from different social class backgrounds. Those who were 'one of us' from working-class backgrounds seemed particularly at ease with their customers. They sometimes lived in the same locality or went to the same bingo hall, shop or church as their customers. They often had mutual friends or acquaintances and knew customers outside of the formal business situation. For example, the daughter of one customer regularly babysat for the collector. Those from slightly higher social classes were slightly more detached from their customers. All the female agents were of a similar age so it is difficult to know whether age would have had an effect independent of gender. The fact that these women were in their 30s and 40s meant that they were the same sorts of ages as many customers.

There was rather greater variation in the personal relationships built up by the male collectors. Although women were better at developing close relationships, the men were full-time workers and tended to spend more time with each customer. They had also been collectors for many years and so had known some customers, as one put it, for *'donkeys years'*. So although there was less general shared experience, the collectors might have been around during major family changes - children being born, the first day at school, partners leaving, serious illnesses, deaths in the family. All of these bound the collector slightly more to the customer.

Two of the male collectors were good at developing close personal relationships. As with the female agents, these two male collectors seemed very relaxed and at home in their customers' houses. They would walk in, immediately sit in an armchair, stroke the dog and talk to the children. Their conversation was also about the customer and their family. A female customer of one collector described what happened when he made his usual call,

> *I know what time he's coming, so normally the kettle's already been boiled and .. he's got a tremendous sweet tooth, so it's normally a piece of cake, sometimes a couple of pieces of cake and different biscuits and so on. Even the kids now, you know, '[He's] walking up the path, mum', so on goes the kettle, you know. Out come the cake tins. The girls do it. It's just the instinct straightaway, straight to the cupboard.*

These collectors also got on well with the male customers. The conversations here tended to be about sport or TV.

Humour was one of the main mechanisms used by these two male collectors to develop relationships with their customers. Although the female collectors did have a laugh with their customers they also had fairly serious conversations. Their male counterparts were much more likely to joke and banter with their customers. One 58 year-old male customer explained,

> *He comes in, sits down, has a chat. He's like an old friend really ... if you've got a problem, he'll listen. He'll have a laugh and a joke, yeah, he's just a nice person, very easy going.*

These two collectors were the most entrepreneurial of all the collectors. The other three male collectors had more of a paternalist streak in them and tended to be more reserved with their customers.

They rarely sat down in customers' houses and would only do so if strongly requested to, perching uncomfortably on the edge of a chair. They did not indulge in bantering to the extent of the other two male collectors. This was true even though they had also been in the business for many years and so had some very long-standing relationships. Their relative distance from their customers seemed to be based on a respect for their customers' privacy and a desire not to invade their personal space. When speaking about their customers, they seemed to have the most genuine respect and concern for their customers than the other collectors. This was part of the 'paternalism' mentioned earlier. One customer described her collector's usual visit,

We normally chat and he tells me about things, about him moving. And we talk about different things, we have a chat on the doorstep. The neighbour next door comes out and says, 'good morning!'

Another described her dealings with another of the more reserved collectors,

I call him in. He just stands at the back of the settee normally. His money's ready for him, I know what day he's coming. He just takes it and ... sometimes we have a chat.

One customer was one of the few who called her collector by his surname even though her relationship with him was relatively close and went back over 25 years.

Mr [Smith] see [my daughter] being born. Well, he didn't actually see her being born, but she was born when he was around ... Mr [Smith], he's never ever aged that man, to me, he's always been the same ... he's very nice, very obliging man.

Although the male collectors generally did not have such close relationships with their customers, their customers often found them easier to get on with than close male relatives. One woman in her 30s remarked,

You can talk to him better than my own father, you can. He's really understanding he is. He comes in and he talks to the children. They like him.

The socio-economic characteristics of customers were also important. Women customers, particularly those in their 30s and 40s, found it easiest to get on well with their collectors, whether male or female. Although these women customers were often the busiest people, they also seemed the most relaxed in terms of relating to others. Male customers, particularly the youngest ones, seemed to have the most formal relationships although some collectors managed to hit on a topic – usually football – which could encourage them into a dialogue.

The socio-economic characteristics of the customers were also important because, as has already been mentioned, the better-off customers were considered more 'valuable' than the poorer ones. So collectors would make more of an effort to develop close relationships with their better-off customers. But the collectors who were from working-class backgrounds had slightly less in common with these customers than those from more upwardly aspiring and achieving backgrounds. So although 'one of us' collectors generally had very close relationships with their customers, this was not always the case.

The nature of the relationship changed over time as customers and collectors got to know each other more. At first, the relationship might be fairly formal and business might take place on the doorstep. But after a while this might change. As one customer recalled,

> *Initially, we'd have a general chat. You know, chit-chat at the door. And then when you get to know [Eric], he'll come in, he'll sit down and even have a cup of tea if he's got the time ... he's more like a friend than anything because we've got similar views on lots of subjects.*

Sometimes customers had known collectors from when they were young and so their personal relationship preceded the business one. Customers whose families had not previously used a moneylender were generally more formal, at least at first, with the moneylender. They had fairly low expectations and so were particularly pleased with the attitude and approach of their collectors.

The closest relationships were therefore between women agents and women customers of a similar age and family situation. In many ways, moneylending is part of a 'women's economy'. The majority of collectors and customers are women and the importance of personal contact may be due to a preference among women for less formal relationships and situations.

Those whose families had used the collector in the past also had strong relationships with their collectors. The most distant relationships were between the 'paternalist' collectors and some of their more recent customers – especially if they were also men.

The power balance

The power balance between customers and collectors could not, of course, be observed directly. It had to be inferred partly from what was said, but also from the objective situation of the customer and collector. Although most relationships were fairly friendly on a personal level, the power balance varied greatly between each one. It depended on three main factors: the income level of the customer, their access to other sources of credit and their need for a loan.

Customers on a relatively high income who could use other types of credit and were using the moneylender to finance the purchase of consumer goods were much more likely to be in control of the relationship than those on a very low income who had no other way of finding money for some essential expenditure.

The high-income customers were more likely to be able to afford to borrow and repay large sums and so were the moneylender's best customers. So the moneylender was very keen for them to stay a customer. But with their access to alternative sources of credit or ability to go without consumer goods, the customers could end the relationship if they did not like the collector or the service provided. So the collector was fairly dependent on these customers.

The power balance tipped the other way with the low-income customers who were borrowing to pay for bills and essentials. These people were much more dependent on the collector. But although these people were most vulnerable and found it difficult to end the relationship, they were of least value to the moneylender because they had little chance of borrowing and repaying large sums.

The power balance also varied at different times in the relationship. At the very start of the relationship, customers had generally been in relatively strong financial situations. But if their circumstances changed and they began a family, became a lone parent or lost their job, their dependence on the moneylender grew. And this was especially true if they had got into a habit of using a moneylender, as many people had. Although some people did stop using a moneylender when times got difficult, many did not. And many particularly appreciated the fact that if difficult times did arise, the moneylender would be there to 'help them out'.

The power balance also shifted at different times within and between loans. When a potential borrower asked for a loan, the collector was in a very strong position and had the power to grant or refuse. But collectors argued that they were not omnipotent, as they were often concerned that refusing someone a loan would lose them a customer. So they sometimes took risks and gave loans which they were not completely happy about. As soon as the customer had been granted credit, the control switched to them. In theory, they had the power to pay or not to pay. If they did not pay, the moneylender could actually do little about that particular loan. The main sanction would be that they would not be able to get credit again from that company. This was a powerful weapon against some of the poorer customers. And most people did pay if they could afford it, but some wielded their power and missed a few payments.

During one of the observation rounds a collector called on a family who had taken out a loan just before going on holiday. They had made no provision for any of the £32 payments during the four weeks they were away and so they now owed £128. The agent told the customer that her line manager had asked her to get more than one week's payment, to make up for some of the missed payments. The customer was not pleased about this and said that she had no intention of paying any more than £32 that week. She complained that the loans were expensive enough anyway so she was not prepared to pay more. The agent asked, fairly meekly, if the customer would consider paying just £1 more a week on top of the £32. But the customer refused. The agent said that her manager would not be too happy about it. The customer replied,

> Tell him to sod off ... I'm paying enough already. I'm not paying any more!

She told the agent to send the manager round if he was unhappy.

The agent was fairly self-controlled during this call, but she was angry when she got back into the car. She felt that she had given the customer a loan in good faith and that they were not sticking to their side of the bargain. They had paid well before getting the loan but as soon as they received the money they missed several payments. The agent had expected them to make some gesture towards making up for the misses. She did not want to show her anger because the couple had been good customers in the past and she did not want to ruin her relationship with them. The line manager would probably make a visit.

In this case, the agent was fairly impotent. There was little she could do to recover the money paid. She did not want to upset the customer who had paid well in the past and so she acted very calmly.

But under this calm surface, she was angry. The tables would turn in the future, but for now, the collector had to grin and bear it.

As a customer came towards the end of a loan, the boot shifted back to the other foot. The customer was now in the hands of the collector who again had the power to decide whether to grant or refuse credit. People generally seemed to pay better as their loan came to an end and they realised that they needed or wanted another loan.

The underlying nature of the relationship
The underlying nature of the relationship reflected how power in the relationship was used. A collector who has control of the relationship may use it to exploit or support their customer.

As has been argued earlier, friendship was sometimes used to manipulate people into borrowing more and repaying better. Customers were sometimes told that their collectors depended on them for their commission. Some customers wanted to help out their friendly and helpful collectors by taking out further loans and keeping up repayments.

Those who were most dependent – on a very low income, lacking access to alternative sources of credit and in desperate need of money – were least likely to be manipulated by the moneylender. Collectors saw little point encouraging such people to borrow more if they did not repay well. And many of these customers were of pension age and so even if they were paying well, the moneylender would try to discourage future loans. If anything, moneylenders tried to reduce the dependence of such customers on them. One exception to this was with people who did repay their loans on time even though they had to make sacrifices to do so. The moneylender was happy to lend to them because they paid on time. The customer made no visible signs of having difficulties because they did not wish to jeopardise their credit-worthiness. There were relatively few customers who came into this category. Most who had difficulties paying did miss payments from time to time, thus signalling to the moneylender to be careful in lending more out.

Many customers found their collector to be helpful and supportive on a personal level. They did not find them threatening or unpleasant.

The image of a moneylender is of a shady lender who exploits their most vulnerable customers through intimidation. The reality of licensed moneylending is more likely to be that of a pleasant collector who may sometimes manipulate their least vulnerable customers through friendship but more often simply provides service with a smile.

As well as looking at the underlying nature of the relationship between moneylender and customer, it is important to remember that there is a relationship between the company and customer. Moneylenders may be providing 'service with a smile' but that service could be making people worse off. So what is at the heart of this relationship? What does it mean to be a customer of a moneylending company? Of course, at the heart of this commercial relationship is the profit-motive. Moneylending companies, like banks and finance houses, aim to make the largest possible profit through maximising the number of customers and then maximising the amount each borrows and repays.

This is understandable since moneylending is a business and not a social service. But these companies are sometimes dealing with the most disadvantaged people and it is this aspect of the business which many critics are most unhappy about. Lending money at 400 per cent APR for someone to buy a non-essential consumer durable is one thing but lending at the same rate for someone to afford the necessities of life is something else. Should companies be able to make profits from people in such circumstances? Whether we think they should or not, it must be remembered that other businesses, for example the local corner shop, will be making profits from the same people. So if moneylenders are exploiting their customers they are just doing the same as other profit-making companies. But the extent of that exploitation, that is the size of the profit, may vary.

Another way of looking at the underlying nature of the relationship between moneylenders and their customers is to turn the question round and ask: What situation would customers be in if moneylending did not exist? In terms of their weekly disposable incomes, it is undoubtedly true that most customers would be better off. But their situation would have changed in other ways too.

Those who had used the moneylender to buy consumer goods would either have been able to use other sources of credit or would have had to go without their 'luxuries'. For example, the customer who bought the CD player had a partner in work and had used HP before. She probably could have bought the CD on credit from a shop. Others would not have been able to finance purchase of a major item. The lone parent who borrowed money for a camcorder is unlikely to have been able to finance this purchase and the pensioner who borrowed money for a foreign holiday would also have had difficulties. So although these people might have been better off each week, they would have gone without something which they wanted. Maybe they would have managed to save, but maybe not.

Those who borrowed money from a moneylender to smooth over the ups and downs in their income would also have been better off each week. But they would have lost the opportunity to buy consumer goods during some of the ups and might have had more difficulties finding money for the necessities during the downs.

Those who used the moneylender to help pay for bills and other essentials would also have been better off each week but they would have lost the security they felt from having a moneylender.

To some extent, these latter two groups preferred to have less spending money each week in order to receive a lump sum every so often. They found it very difficult to save and so would not have been able to manage their money in this way without the moneylender.

The root of the problems facing these people was their poverty. This poverty resulted in a lack of access to other, cheaper forms of credit and caused difficulties in maintaining an adequate standard of living. Use of a moneylender was often a consequence rather than a cause of these people's problems.

Of course, if licensed moneylending did not exist, people might turn to unlicensed lenders for a similar service. Although this research did not include unlicensed lenders, hearsay evidence suggests that at least some of these lenders have even higher interest rates and use less subtle methods when dealing with their customers.

So, generally, current customers gained something, and *felt* that they gained something, from their use of a moneylender. They either gained the ability to purchase consumer goods or to receive a lump sum every so often or, more intangibly, they gained the security of knowing that they could manage on their money. This feeling of regularity and sometimes security was much more a feature of the relationship than was uncertainty or fear, as is characterised in the popular image of moneylending. Customers did not dread the weekly knock at the door, nor did they particularly look forward to it – it was simply a way of life.

KEY POINTS

- At a time when 'relationship banking' is on the decline, licensed moneylending continues to rely heavily on personal contact between lender and borrower.

- On a personal level, relationships are often very informal and friendly. Women agents in particular have close relationships with women customers.

- The power balance within the relationship depends on the income level of the customer, their access to other types of credit and their need for a loan.

- The feeling of regularity or security is much more a feature of the relationship between moneylenders and their customers than uncertainty or fear.

---

7 Conclusions and Policy Implications

The aim of this research was to provide an independent assessment of the licensed moneylending, or weekly collected credit, industry. The main conclusion is that, while the industry's view of itself is too rosy, it is a more accurate picture than that of the media and critics of the industry.

By and large, customers of moneylenders are happy with the service they receive and are not exploited by the companies. Where customers do have financial difficulties, these are generally due to low income rather than use of a moneylender.

At the heart of the relationship between a moneylender and customer is a mutual dependence. The moneylender would not be in business without the customer and the customer would not be able to borrow without the lender. This dependence mainly varies according to the income of the customer, their access to other forms of credit and their need for money. To some extent, those customers who are most dependent are of least 'value' to the moneylender and so will not be encouraged to borrow too much.

The personal nature of the relationship between collector and customer is one of the main features of moneylending. Contrary to the media stereotype, licensed moneylenders use friendship rather than fear to increase custom. But although licensed moneylenders are not threatening and intimidating borrowers, the opportunity exists for them to manipulate their customers or encourage them to borrow more than they would do otherwise. People may be particularly vulnerable to pressure when in their own homes – which is one reason why doorstep canvasssing of cash loans is illegal. The research did not find evidence of extensive manipulation or encouragement to borrow but the opportunity exists and it is difficult to know how such relationships can be regulated since, by their very nature, they develop in private.

In some respects, the moneylending business is part of a 'women's economy'. Most collectors are women as are their customers. The informal, home-centred nature of the business may well be a reflection of its gender-specific nature. As we saw in the first chapter, illegal moneylenders in the past were often poor women lending to friends and neighbours who were even poorer than themselves. And leaving philanthropists aside, moneylending tended to evolve as a working-class solution to the working-class problem of poverty. What is interesting, if not depressingly familiar, is that the two companies included in this study which had been started by working-class people, had both been started by working-class *men*. It seems that although women may be heavily involved in the moneylending industry they do so as part-time agents and seldom have the opportunities or resources to build up a business. And although some women customers are taken on as agents, few seem to move up the ranks in existing companies.

This chapter begins by giving an independent assessment of licensed moneylending before focusing on some particular aspects of the industry which warrant further discussion. It ends by looking outside the industry to the ways in which low-income consumers could be given more choice about the credit they use.

An independent assessment of moneylending

We began, in chapter 1, by outlining two views of moneylending – the critics' view and the industry's own view. We return to these views in light of this research.

Doorstep lending and collection

Doorstep lending and collection is a central aspect of moneylending. At a time when 'relationship banking' is becoming increasingly rare in the mainstream credit world, the moneylending industry continues to rely heavily on weekly face-to-face contact. The industry claims that this enables them to provide credit to people who can manage the repayments but who would be considered too high a risk by other lenders. Critics of moneylending argue that doorstep lending and collection enables companies to persuade people both to borrow more than they can afford and also to lean on them when they cannot pay.

Doorstep collection *does* improve the moneylender's assessment of ability to repay as they can gather a great deal of information about the customer's situation. But face-to-face contact is also used by moneylenders to assess willingness to pay. Even those on very low incomes may be considered for small amounts of credit if they are thought willing to repay the instalments on time.

Personal contact also provides an opportunity for moneylenders to encourage people to take out further loans. Some moneylenders are too pushy and some customers do stop using them. Moneylenders say they use their greatest persuasive skills on their better-off customers and discourage their poorer customers from taking out a loan. But, nevertheless, many customers have difficulty making their repayments and yet are continually lent further loans. In one respect, people are being given a chance to retain access to credit even though they are very poor. But in another, people are being allowed or encouraged to struggle with repayments which they cannot really afford.

Doorstep collection is an efficient way of collecting repayments and one which customers are keen on. Many customers who are living on low incomes are continually forced to juggle their money. If no-one came to collect their repayments at a particular time in the week there would be a great temptation to dip into the money when they ran short. Few would be able to send off the money on time every week or pay it into a post office. It is also convenient for many people, for example those with several young children or those with mobility difficulties.

There was no evidence in this study of licensed moneylenders using intimidation, threats or violence to extract payment. Little was said or done if people missed payments, although subtle ways of encouraging the customer to repay were sometimes used. For the most part, the relationship between collectors and customers was friendly and the weekly knock on the door simply became part of the routine of life – neither feared nor particularly welcomed.

To sum up, doorstep collection is a central part of moneylending. Its chief importance lies in ensuring that people repay their instalments and therefore keep open access to what is often the only form of legal credit available to them. This face-to-face contact does give moneylenders the potential to try and encourage further borrowing. They generally encourage those who can afford to repay but nevertheless continue to lend to some people who cannot.

The cost of credit

Critics argue that credit from a moneylender is extortionate, partly because of the very high APRs charged. The industry claims that the APR system exaggerates the apparent cost of small, short-term loans and that their high APRs also have to reflect the high costs of doorstep lending and collection.

The APR calculation is not designed to be biased against short-term loans but, since there are fixed costs associated with loans, smaller loans will inevitably be more expensive than larger ones. Although the APR does have various limitations as a means of comparing different types of credit it is still the best measure currently available.

Moneylending *is* much more expensive than other types of credit. The APRs typically vary between 100 to 500 per cent depending principally on the length of the loan. The APR on a bank or building society loan will be around 20 per cent but these are generally only available for large sums of money – £500 or above so direct comparisons are often difficult.

Moneylending may be more expensive than other types of credit, but *how much* more expensive? Is it extortionate? It is difficult to draw a line above which an APR becomes extortionate and below which it is not. The arguments against such a ceiling are that it might encourage lenders to set rates at or near the ceiling when they could be lower. And depending on where the ceiling is set, legal moneylenders might be unable to trade profitably in the market, thus reducing access of low-income families to legal forms of credit. The OFT has considered introducing a threshold or a range of thresholds but decided against doing so because of the difficulties (OFT 1991).

This research suggests that the cost of credit from a licensed moneylender does not justify the label 'extortionate' as there is no evidence of violence, threats of violence or the use of grossly unfair methods of persuasion. But there is some evidence that the strong personal relationships between collectors and customers do encourage a habit and state of dependence and customers can be manipulated.

Although the interest charged on credit from a moneylender is not extortionate, it is extremely high. This is partly because customers have fairly limited access to other forms of credit and so have little choice but to pay dearly for credit. There is also evidence that customers do not fully understand and compare the costs of credit through using the APR. Many customers were aware that moneylending was expensive but they did not know the APR relating to their loan. They focused on the amount borrowed, the amount charged and the weekly repayment. They were aware, however, that other creditors levied default charges which could make such forms of credit very expensive. The issue of consumer information is considered again later in this chapter.

Moneylending is also expensive because of the cost of doorstep collection. The industry estimates that the overall cost of providing this service is between one third and one half of the total charges.

The high cost of credit from a moneylender is also due to the fact that some customers take longer to pay than the contractually-agreed amount of time. Although defaulters will be paying a lower real rate of charge than the contractually-agreed rate, the overall cost of credit will take this into account and so those who pay on time will be subsidising the bad payers.

Although some customers take longer to repay a loan than the contracually-agreed time, others renew a loan early. Moneylenders are often criticised for these renewals or top-up loans since the effective APRs can sometimes run into four figures. This issue is addressed in the next section of this chapter as is the issue of 'First payments' which is where the first repayment of a loan is taken out from the amount lent at the time of initially lending the money.

To sum up, the costs of credit from a moneylender are extremely high and much higher than most other types of credit. These costs are mainly due to the expense of doorstep collection and the high risks attached to lending to people on low and unstable incomes. It is likely that even if companies ran their businesses to break even rather than make a profit, the costs of credit from a moneylender would still be very high.

Default charges

Critics claim that moneylenders add on extra charges if people default, thus adding to their debt problems. The industry denies this.

Default charges are very rarely levied even though some customers take longer than the specified period to repay their loans. The costs of this are included in the basic loan charge. Thus the good payers are subsidising the bad ones.

It may seem unfair that this subsidisation takes place. While redistribution may be seen as socially valuable in some settings, none of these customers were particularly well off. So the redistribution was from the poor to the even poorer. One company overcame this problem by offering a discounted interest rate to good payers. They offered a 16 week loan at an APR of 215 per cent to *'customers able to pay the exact terms'* and a 28 week loan at an APR of 259 per cent to others.

Customers' access to other types of credit

Both the critics and the industry agree that moneylending customers have little access to other forms of credit. But whereas critics conclude that this enables companies to exploit customers' dependence, the industry believes that they are providing a valuable service to people who are excluded by mainstream creditors.

Customers *do* have limited access to other forms of credit because of their generally poor economic circumstances. And so, to some extent, the discussion about APRs is academic – people do not have the opportunity to shop around for cheap cash loans. Their main option is between using a moneylender or going without, or in some cases, saving. Once customers begin to use a moneylender they often get into a habit of borrowing and so no longer consciously even make a choice between using or not using one.

Moneylending companies face little competition from other creditors, with the exception of mail order. And the extent of competition between moneylending companies is open to debate – a debate which we will return to later in this chapter.

The financial situations of customers

There is a perception that all moneylending customers are in desperate financial situations which become worse through use of a moneylender. The industry asserts that they are not interested in lending to people in dire financial straits and that their customers come from most walks of life.

Few people were in desperate financial situations when they first became a customer of a moneylender, as lenders tried to recruit people in stable financial and family situations. But many people suffered a downturn in their finances while they were customers. As long as they continued to pay, the moneylender was not too concerned about their circumstances. If they did miss payments, the moneylender accepted a certain level of default and sometimes tried to reduce the amount they borrowed.

Some customers used a moneylender to enable them to purchase consumer goods. Some used a moneylender to smooth over the ups and downs of irregular income. Others, particularly the pensioners, used loans from the moneylender to help them manage money and pay for essentials such as bills.

People did get into a habit of borrowing from a moneylender, but this was not generally a downward spiral of debt. Both customer and moneylender sought to find a level of borrowing which could be maintained. In some cases, however, that level was difficult to maintain.

Although some people would have preferred not to have needed to use a moneylender, they saw their main problem as not having enough money to live on. Current customers did not feel that their financial problems were caused by use of a moneylender.

The risk of default
There is general agreement that moneylending customers have a high risk of default but critics believe this is because lenders do not adequately assess ability to repay. The lenders say that default is more a result of the drops in income which their customers are prone to.

Information about default is not available on an industry-wide level but evidence from the companies suggests that about a quarter of customers miss payments in any given week. So there is a high risk of default among moneylenders' customers. This is mainly due to the difficult and unpredictable financial circumstances which face customers. Moneylenders advance credit fully anticipating that many of their customers will miss at least some repayments. But as long as this default is at a fairly low level, it is not considered a problem by the moneylenders. It may, however, be a problem for the customers.

The weekly visit usually ensures that any difficulties are identified by the collector at an early stage and a suitable level of repayments is arranged. The problem of non-contact is a regular headache for other creditors.

Regulating the moneylending industry
The main conclusion must be that the licensed moneylending industry as a whole does not involve *'deceitful or oppressive'* practices and so

does not come within the bounds of *'socially harmful lending'* (OFT 1991). The industry is generally being regulated and is regulating itself in such a way that most customers do not encounter any serious problems. But there are some aspects of the industry which warrant further discussion.

Competition within the industry

As we have seen, customers of moneylenders have limited access to other sources of credit, apart from mail order. The industry acknowledges this point but argues that customers have a great deal of choice between different moneylending firms. Critics argue that one of the reasons for the high cost of credit is the lack of competition within the sector.

It was not one of the original aims of the research to assess the industry as a whole and comment on the amount of competition within it. Nevertheless, certain findings are relevant. The research showed that the collectors were often concerned about turning someone down for a loan in case they lost that customer to another company. But customers, generally, were extremely conservative preferring the 'devil' they knew. They prefered to stay with the collector they knew unless there were serious problems. And in any case, companies offered broadly similar products at fairly similar prices and so there was often little to choose between them.

Since customers developed loyalty to a particular collector rather than a company, there is a danger that companies could try to increase their customer base by 'poaching' collectors from other companies. Companies try to prevent this by including restrictive covenants in their agents' contracts. These clauses are designed to prevent agents taking customers with them if they leave one company for another. But courts will only enforce such clauses if they are considered *reasonable* in scope and duration.

Although there are about 1200 licensed moneylending companies, only 6 are national and 50-60 are regionally based. So within each locality, people have a relatively limited choice. It should be remembered however, that the bank and building society sector is also dominated by a few giants.

The CCA receives membership applications from about 50 new traders a year. About a quarter of these are businesses which are in the process of being built up totally from scratch. Because of the conservatism of customers, any new business will take a great deal of investment in time and money before it becomes profitable.

There was some indication of local networking and cooperation between companies in terms of credit referencing. This is not to say that there were complex local monopolies but competition was not quite as aggressive and cut-throat as some might argue.

The evidence suggests that although there is some competition between companies, it may be limited. More research is needed on this issue.

Marketing of loans

It is illegal for companies to canvas cash loans on the doorstep. If a potential new customer sees an advert and wants a loan, they will contact the company. The company then has to send a letter to the potential customer and have a document signed before they can visit the customer in their own home. In this way, the law tries to ensure that the initiative for a loan always comes from the customer because it is much easier to pressurise people to take out a loan when speaking to them face-to-face than it is through advertisements and direct mail marketing.

Although this procedure is generally thought to safeguard consumers' interests there are some occasions where an ex-customer or a friend of a current customer would like a cash loan but has to go through the procedure even though they may know the collector and know exactly what they want. In this case, the initiative for the loan is coming from the customer rather than from the collector, but the customer still has to go through the formal procedure. The industry and some regulators feel that such a procedure is unnecessarily bureaucratic in these cases. But if the regulations were to be amended they should be changed in such a way that the spirit of the old regulations is maintained so that the opportunity for pressurising people is limited.

Since canvassing cash loans is illegal, companies try to recruit new customers through canvassing goods. Several collectors were critical of canvassers for selling items to people who did not subsequently repay. Some people found canvassers very pushy and refused to deal with them but people with little money may find it difficult to resist the pressure to buy something on the doorstep and then may have problems paying for it.

So while moneylenders generally do not encourage people to borrow unless they can afford and are willing to repay, canvassers do not follow the same rules. This is a general problem in the credit industry where there is often a conflict between increasing the number of customers and ensuring ability to repay.

Managers in moneylending companies should review the methods used by, and the motivations of, their canvassers. Canvassers who are pushy can deter potential customers. And those who succeed in selling to customers who cannot afford to pay cause difficulties for those customers and for the collectors who have to visit them every week to try and recover the money.

Once a moneylender has a foothold with a new customer they then have the opportunity to use various techniques to encourage further borrowing. The research showed that this opportunity was not generally exploited and customers stopped using pushy moneylenders. But the opportunity is there and is a source of concern since it is not easy to see how such situations could be regulated.

Documentation and consumer information

Providing useful and accessible information to consumers can only help them make better decisions. The CCA have drawn up several standard documents in consultation with regulators. These documents give information to the customer and conform to the letter of the law. They have also been reviewed as part of the plain English campaign.

But it is well known that consumers rarely read any contract in detail before signing. Certainly, the customers of moneylenders interviewed in this study seldom read any of the forms they were given or sent. Most used their payment book as their record of the money previously borrowed and currently owing. Others rarely looked even at that and just trusted their collector to let them know when their loan was at an end.

Although people cannot be forced to read all the literature, and indeed some people are unable to read, they could be encouraged to look at the most important messages if forms are designed to be simple and draw attention to particular aspects. This is a general problem with all legal contracts and research is needed into the design of such documents. In this context, it may be useful for the industry and its regulators to look again at the forms which are used in order to improve consumers' understanding of the contract they are entering into.

This research confirms previous work which shows that people on low incomes make rational decisions and act rationally, given the circumstances they find themselves in. Moneylending customers are no different from other consumers of credit in their understanding of the costs and conditions of loans. The issues such as the APR and the implications of renewing a loan early are very complex ones for all consumers to understand. Along with the APR, other, simpler ways of providing comparative costs of credit should be developed so that all consumers can make more informed decisions.

First payments

'First payments' are where a company makes a loan to a customer and takes out the first payment at the time the loan is made. So when the moneylender leaves the customer's house, the customer has less in their hand than the amount they have officially borrowed.

Only some companies remove the first payment from the original loan. Others wait until they return the following week to take out the first repayment. The companies that do remove first payments justify the practice by saying that most of their customers borrow money on a Thursday or Friday and that the first repayment is due, according to the contract, by the end of that week – that is, the Saturday. Rather than have a collector make a special visit to collect that payment – which would increase the cost – the collector takes the payment at the time the loan is made.

Whatever the legal position of first payments, many customers and some collectors, dislike the practice and see it as unfair. For this reason if no other, the companies which currently use the procedure should review it.

Refinancing and rebates

Refinancing is the practice whereby the balance due under an old loan is paid off with part of a new loan. Top-up loans and renewals are other terms for refinancing. This aspect of moneylending is greatly criticised as the effective APRs of some renewals are extremely high – probably in four figures in some cases.

The industry defends itself by arguing that refinancing is common to other types of credit – for example when owner-occupiers move house they refinance rather then take out a second mortgage. The industry also argues that the pressure for renewals comes from the customer rather than the company.

The research highlighted some company rules or guidelines about refinancing. For example, some companies will only refinance once the customer has paid off more than a certain proportion of the original loan. And customers are legally entitled to rebates which are applied to the unearned interest on the old loan.

But such statutory rebates often give little money back to the customer. For example, if a customer borrowed £300 at an agreed rate of £14.70 a week over 29 weeks, but actually repaid it over 20 weeks, they would be entitled to a rebate of just 29 pence. This statutory rebate is small for two reasons. Firstly, as with other credit repayments such as mortgages, a high proportion of early repayments is interest. This means that, towards the end of the loan, there is often little unearned interest to be repaid. Secondly, the administrative costs of renewing a loan are passed on to the customer through an '8 week deferral' rule. This means that if a customer settles a loan 7 weeks before the end of the loan, they will not be entitled to any rebate. If they settle 9 weeks before the end of a loan, they will be entitled to the equivalent of 1 week's rebate.

Some companies offer more than the statutory rebate, particularly on very short-term loans.

There was some evidence from the research that customers who were struggling with repayments were discouraged from renewing early but other customers were often informed at the earliest point in their repayment cycle that they could renew if they wanted to. One company printed a receipt for customers on which they also displayed the amount of money that customers could borrow should they wish to renew or take out another loan at that point.

Some moneylending customers are in very difficult financial situations and the merest suggestion or knowledge that they can renew a loan will encourage them to do so. Collectors are also under pressure to do as much business as possible and so may encourage some people to renew. Although the statutory rebate system technically prevents interest being charged on interest, the way it works in practice means that little is returned and the effective APRs of renewal loans are extremely high. The statutory rebate system, particularly the 8 week deferral period, should be reviewed. And moneylending companies should review their policies and practice on refinancing.

Increasing choice for low-income borrowers

Although the licensed moneylending industry is working in a generally satisfactory manner, many customers are living on low incomes and have limited access to other types of credit. The final section of this chapter assesses ways of increasing choice for low-income borrowers.

Use of consumer credit became widespread over the 1980s and went hand-in-hand, perhaps even fuelling, greater expectations of a consumer lifestyle. But over the same period, there was a growth in poverty and inequality. As a consequence, many people were left living in a consumer society with their aspirations raised but with limited access to mainstream credit which might enable them to achieve some of those aspirations.

It is among this group of people that the customers of moneylenders are drawn. Some customers use moneylending because their financial and other circumstances are such that they would be most unlikely to have access to most other sources of credit. Others, however, have used other sources of credit particularly when times are better, but stopped doing so when their circumstances change (see Kempson et al 1994). For these people, the attraction of using a moneylender rather than retaining an overdraft or a credit card was the increased control they felt they had over their money. In a sense, they had restricted their access to mainstream credit sources because they were considered inappropriate for their needs.

Customers of moneylenders are therefore either excluded from mainstream credit sources or exclude themselves because they consider such sources unsuitable.

Although the customers of licensed moneylenders are generally receiving low incomes, they are not amongst the poorest people in Britain. The very poorest will not be considered credit-worthy even by a licensed moneylender. This research did not include such people but they are a cause for concern as they may be excluded from all licensed forms of credit, and may turn instead to illegal lenders.

Other sources, such as mail order, credit unions and the social fund may be available both to moneylending customers and also to those not considered credit-worthy even by licensed moneylenders.

Mail order is used by many moneylending customers. But this is only an alternative to buying goods on credit or borrowing from a moneylender to buy goods which could otherwise have been bought through a mail order catalogue. The successful growth of the mail order industry in the last 20 years may well be one reason for the shift to cash loans which many moneylending firms have had to make over that period. Those moneylending firms which continue to sell goods on credit usually have lower rates of interest on goods than they do on cash loans. This is partly because the interest can be hidden in the price of goods. Mail order companies may also hide their interest charges in higher prices and indeed many customers commented on the expense of goods from mail order sources. So mail order is an alternative to moneylending but a limited one.

Credit unions have been heralded by some as the way of providing a low-cost alternative to moneylending. But credit unions have not taken off in this country. This research suggests that there are two main limitations to credit unions providing low-cost credit for people with little or no alternative. The first is the requirement to save with a credit union before taking out a loan. The very difficulty of saving on a low income is often the reason why people both start and continue to borrow from a moneylender. The second problem is that there is no doorstep collection service with a credit union. Payments are usually taken in to the local office. It is likely that many of those who currently use a moneylender would not keep up repayments without doorstep collection or some other method such as direct payment from benefits or wages. With better funding and the reforms which are currently underway, credit unions could begin to help more people. But their role seems likely to be somewhat limited.

The social fund is almost the last resort for many people who are unable to provide basic items for themselves and their families. This source may be used by those who have little access to a moneylender. Its problems are well-known from the previous research (Huby and Dix among others) which continues to be ignored by the government. The main problems relate to the cash-limited, discretionary nature of the system along with its restriction to certain groups, such as those on income support. It is also restricted to certain needs, such as the need for a cooker or bedding. The system involves a great deal of paperwork which will deter all except the most needy. But the most needy may be considered 'too poor' to be given a loan if they already have substantial deductions being taken out of their benefit.

As well as reforming credit unions and the social fund, other methods of providing 'social loans' have been considered. For example, in the Netherlands, there are municipal banks which provide subsidised loans. These seem unlikely to be developed in Britain at the moment because of the set-up costs and the need for continued government subsidisation. But in any case, they do not seem to be reaching the types of people who currently use or are excluded from licensed moneylending.

One suggestion has been that other organisations, such as the Post Office or supermarkets, could take on a social lending role under a system of franchises. To meet the two criteria of lender control and need for subsidy, it has been proposed that loans might be linked to benefit or wage payments. Social security benefits could be paid through Automated Cash Transfer (ACT) to the franchise organisation who would then make cash payments to benefit recipients. One requirement of the franchise would be that part of the interest that the organisation would receive on such large sums of money should be used to subsidise the cost of providing loans to the people who 'bank' with them. Repayments could be deducted at source from the 'account' in order to prevent arrears accruing (Kempson 1993).

Such a system has its merits but organisations such as the Post Office have no track record in making decisions about credit. Rules would have to be stipulated, for example, about the proportion of benefit which could be deducted as repayments, so that people did not leave themselves with too little to live on. These problems are not insurmountable and the idea deserves further thought and development.

In conclusion
Our overall conclusion is that legal moneylending, or weekly collected credit, provides a valuable service to a section of the population that most other creditors would not lend to. But there are specific practices that need addressing to reduce the risk of people being exploited by their lack of choice. And there are very high rates of charge for the service.

As is so often the case, the poor are paying more. This is because lending to people with a high risk of default is very costly. Door-to-door collection is necessary but expensive. And allowing people to take longer than the originally agreed term to pay a loan will increase the overall costs. It is likely that, even if companies made no profits, the cost of weekly collected credit would still be very high.

And even if the market is perfectly regulated, it will not be able to provide cheap credit to low-income families without some form of subsidy.

Reforms of the social fund and greater government encouragement for credit unions would improve the situation for low-income borrowers. But such changes, on their own, would probably only be of marginal help. Further investigation is needed into ways of increasing access to low-cost credit, for example, by developing existing ideas about social lending. Moneylenders' customers, along with those excluded from legal moneylending, should have access to affordable and suitable credit.

It should be remembered, however, that poverty is the underlying reason why some people lack access to suitable, low-cost credit. The improved provison of social lending schemes will be a help. But, to some extent, these schemes will just be papering over the cracks of the much more fundamental problem of poverty.

Bibliography

Association of Metropolitan Authorities (1994) *The expansion of credit unions*, AMA

Aristotle (1957) *The politics*, Penguin

Becker, H (1970) *Sociological work*, Aldine

Berthoud, R (1991) 'The social fund – is it working?' in *Policy Studies*, vol 12.1

Berthoud, R and Hinton, C (1989) *Credit Unions*, PSI

Berthoud, R and Kempson, E (1992) *Credit and debt: the PSI report*, PSI

Braudel, F (1973) *Capitalism and material life 1400-1800* Fontana/Collins

Burgess, R (1984) *In the field*, Allen and Unwin

Caplovitz, D (1967) *The poor pay more*, Free Press

Consumer Credit Association UK (1992) *Mirage or reality*, CCA

Daly, M and Walsh, J (1988) *Money-lending and low income families*, Combat Poverty Agency

Duncan, S and Kirby, K (1983) *Preventing rent arrears*, HMSO

Esser, H (1993) 'The rationality of everyday behaviour', in *Rationality and Society,* vol 5 no. 1

Goode, R (1994) *Guide to the consumer credit act 1974*, Butterworth

Hammersley, M and Atkinson, P (1983) *Ethnography: Principles in practice*, Tavistock

Huby M and Dix, G (1992) *Evaluating the social fund*, HMSO

Kempson, E (1994) *Outside the banking system*, HMSO

Kempson, E, Bryson, A, and Rowlingson, K (1994) *Hard Times? How poor families make ends meet*, PSI

National Consumer Council (1983) *Banking services and the consumer*, Methuen

National Consumer Council (1994) *Saving for credit: the future of credit unions in Britain*, JRF

Office of Fair Trading (1991) *Unjust credit transactions*, OFT

Office of Fair Trading (1993) *Consultation document on the working and enforcement of the consumer credit act 1974*, OFT

Office of Fair Trading (1994) *Consumer credit deregulation*, OFT

Pember Reeves, M (1979 - first published 1913) *Round about a pound a week*, Virago

Rock, P (1973) *Making People Pay*, Routledge and Kegan Paul

Rowlingson, K and Kempson, E (1994) *Paying with plastic: a study of credit card debt*, PSI

Schatzmann, L and Strauss, A (1973) *Field research: Strategies for a natural sociology*, Prentice-Hall

Schultz, A (1964) 'The problem of rationality in the social world', in *Collected papers volume 2*, Martinus Nijhoff

Smith, D and Grey, J (1983) *Police and people in London*, PSI

Tebbutt, M (1983) *Making Ends Meet: Pawnbroking and working-class credit*, St Martin's Press

Vesselitsky, V and Bulkley, M (1917) 'Money-lending among the London poor', in *Sociological Review, vol IX*

Whyte, W (1955) *Street corner society*, University of Chicago Press

Appendix 1

A Day in the Life of a Moneylender

A Friday one summer ...

11.50 We set out from the local office on time but there is quite a lot of traffic in town so the agent is a bit late when she arrives at the first call.

11.55 A woman opens the door with her young children standing around her. She tells the agent that she has not seen her estranged husband recently and so has no money with which to pay. She says this in a very 'matter-of-fact' tone and does not seem concerned about the fact that she is not paying anything. Nor does she seem concerned about how the agent might react. The agent shows slight disappointment and irritation. She smiles at, and is friendly with, the children.

When she gets back into the car the agent says that these people had originally been good customers. He had been in work and they had each had loan accounts. But he lost his job and they stopped paying any money. The line manager visited them and they agreed to pay £2 a week. The husband has now left his wife and children and she rarely even pays the £2 a week. One of the loans was in her name but the woman does not accept responsibility for the loan and only pays it if her husband gives her the money for it. They currently owe about £1,000. The agent and the line manager are sceptical about whether the husband has really left his wife. The line manager will visit this customer to see what else can be done to encourage repayment. The agent shows more irritation once in the car.

12.00 A fairly straightforward call not far from the last. Money picked up and written down in the book.

12.10 Still on the same 1950s council estate. A woman, probably in her 50s, opens the door and starts chatting to the agent. She has recently been harrassed by two local 14 year-old girls. This has distressed her and she has visited the girls' parents. The agent tells her that she should not have to put up with it and is generally sympathetic to the woman. The woman is selling lottery tickets and the agent buys one from her.

12.20 After three fairly clustered calls there is now a little drive out of town into the country. We drive to a very large house, high on a hill. It is owned by a titled family. But the customer is not one of the owners. It is the gardener who lives on the estate. The agent has rarely seen this customer. He was transferred to her from another agent. He leaves his money in the letterbox for her to collect when she arrives. But it is not always there. 'Will it be there today?' thinks the agent. It is not and neither is the gardener. Another case for the line manager to pursue. The agent thinks about the commission that she is losing.

12.30 Back into town. Some large houses, probably not council. A woman in her 60s opens the door and the agent goes into the front room, as usual. The husband takes the dog out for a walk and passes the time of the day with the agent, but no more. He has nothing to do with his wife's finances and does not have a loan with the company. The son and daughter have had loans in the past but the daughter has now moved away from home.

The woman has been a customer for quite some time and she has a fairly close relationship with her agent. Last week she asked to take out a loan and today the agent has all the paperwork and the cash. The agent filled out most of the forms for the customer because she knows, off by heart, the name and address of the woman's employer and her approximate earnings. She double-checks that these have not changed since the last loan. Very little is said about the formalities of the loan. The woman has taken out many loans before and so any conversation is on a more personal level about families and work.

1.15 Since the last call, there have been a couple more calls, including a loan for £100 to one customer. We are still on one side of town. The next visit is to a couple with children. It is the summer holidays and the house is in a semi-chaotic state. The children are playing cluedo on the floor of the living-room and there are lots of toys scattered around. Father is also sitting in the room and there are wet clothes being dried on a clothes horse. The TV is on. The woman invites the agent in, but the agent does not sit down. The woman is thinking about buying some vouchers so that she can get some Christmas presents for the children in the summer sales. She whispers slightly so as not to be overheard. The agent gives her a leaflet with details about the shops covered by the different vouchers.

On the way out, the woman asks the agent how her brother is. The agent's brother has a serious illness. The agent appreciates the concern of the customer but says later that the customer always asks her and this only serves to remind her of his condition. She had not meant to tell the customer about her brother but she had been upset once when he was particularly ill and ended up by telling the customer all about it.

1.30 We buy a sandwich from a local shop and eat it in the car. It is raining now.

2.00 The agent always has a cup of coffee in the next house. The customer is an elderly woman who is not very mobile and sleeps in the living room. She has been a customer for quite some time and has nine children. Her husband left her some time ago when her youngest children were still at home.

She likes to pay off her loans quickly and was disappointed when the company stopped offering shorter-term loans. She makes a comment to the agent about the high level of interest. She pays £140 today to get her loan down quickly. Two of her adult daughters are also present. One has recently had her birthday and there is much talk about the presents she recieved. One brother had forgotten to send a card. The daughters tease the agent because she had not sent a card or remembered the birthday.

The atmosphere in the house is very relaxed and conversation covered many issues from the benefits of shopping alone to new forms of contraception.

2.40   Another fairly elderly woman but much more mobile than the previous customer. The door is opened by her grandson who invites the agent in. The woman's husband had died about a year ago and she is still grieving for him. She speaks to the agent about it and is almost in tears. They talk about her children and grandchildren most of whom the agent has met or knows about. Later, in the car, the agent says that she does not know what to say to this woman and that she finds it difficult to get away sometimes.

3.05   A couple more calls since the last one. There is no reply at one of the calls and the others are fairly straightforward doorstep calls. There are six accounts at the next call. The husband was off work sick last week, what will be the situation now? His wife opens the door and the agent just steps into the hallway. She tells the agent that he is still off work and so cannot pay the £48 which he owes each week. He is only receiving about £80 a week while he is off sick and the rent is £40 a week. The agent advises them to claim housing benefit but the woman hopes that her husband will be back at work soon and thinks that it would take a long time to get any housing benefit. The account is now in arrears by £96. The line manager will probably call to try and arrange reduced payments.

The agent is sympathetic to the couple. They have been good customers in the past and she trusts that he is 'genuinely' sick.

3.10   At the next call, the agent has to be careful to avoid the woman's husband since he does not know that his wife uses a moneylender. If his car is outside, the agent cannot go in. But there is no sign of him today and so the agent approaches. The woman pays £7 instead of the £7.50 she should be paying. This slightly irritates the agent who would prefer the customer to round up rather than round down.

3.13   The agent goes into the next house and sits down with a couple of elderly women. They talk about the extra costs associated with their health conditions. They have an electric fire on even though it is relatively warm. An elderly man, who is 'a friend' of one of the women appears at the door with his dog. The agent tries to beat a hasty retreat. On the way out the man puts his arms around her and touches her in a way which makes her visibly uncomfortable. When she gets back into the car she is quite angry. She dislikes having to put up with this behaviour but she does not want to stop serving the female customer. So she tries to take avoiding action and her husband usually accompanies her on her rounds and makes his presence felt when she visits that particular house.

3.17   The account at this call is in arrears and the customers have now arranged to pay reduced amounts fortnightly when they get their benefit cheque.

3.20   A woman answers the door and asks the agent to come back later as her husband is not home from work yet. The agent agrees but she is not too happy because it is awkward to rearrange times. She sometimes forgets to make these call-backs and she feels this gives the customers an excuse not to pay her.

3.21   In the same street she visits another house. A man opens the door. He is friendly but does not invite the agent in. He gives her the books and the agent takes them back to the car to fill them in. She does not like filling in books out in the open because of the security risks. She drops the books back through his letter box.

3.25   Nearby in the street the agent bumps into another customer. This woman lives close to her sister who is also a customer. The woman has given her repayment money to her sister so that the agent only has to make one visit but the sister is not always in when the agent calls. The agent tells this woman about this and the woman apologises for her sister. The woman also tells the agent that her sister often goes out and leaves her young children on their own. Recently the young son hit the daughter over the head with a hammer. There is general concern about the family.

3.30   At this call, the agent usually receives a reduced amount – often just £1 or £2. This time, however, the customer explains that it is her daughter's 21st birthday so she cannot even afford £1. The agent says very little to the woman but shows her disappointment. Back in the car she is rather more angry than disappointed. The agent thinks that payment to her comes bottom of any list of priorities.

3.35   This is a call-back from yesterday when there was no reply to the agent's knock. This time the door opens ... but it is the customer's 16 year old daughter. The daughter says that she has not seen her mother for some time and has no idea where she is. It is quite common for her to disappear for days at a time. The daughter and agent agree that the woman is probably in the pub. The agent asks the daughter to get her mother to call her. The daughter is happy to do so but says that she is going off to Wales for a holiday and so might not see her mother.

The agent feels sorry for the daughter and her mother. She knows that her mother has had a difficult life and that she now has a drink problem.

3.40   Another busy household. Mum and dad, two adult daughters and a baby grand-daughter. The baby is centre stage. All the adults in the house are customers. The parents take out a loan to decorate the house because one of their daughters is going away on holiday with the baby so it is a good time to decorate. The agent gets on very well with the family and has seen the daughters grow up. Quite a bit of time is spent chatting and filling out the appropriate forms.

4.20   A call to a woman in sheltered housing. The woman's son is visiting her at the time the agent arrives. They chat for while. The woman's daughter is also an agent for the same company.

4.35   On her way to the next call, the agent bumps into another customer in the street. The woman informs the agent that she might not be in next Friday at the regular time. They rearrange a time for Thursday. The agent is pleased to be told in advance that someone is going to be away but she dislikes having to rearrange her calls. The women chat for a while in the street.

4.40   A doorstep call to a male customer. He tells her the local gossip about a recent mugging. The local grapevine had identified the offenders and the word had gone round.

4.50   The agent goes into the living-room in the next call. At home is a female customer and her adult son. He has severe learning difficulties. The DSS has recently said that he no longer counts as sick or disabled and so has to claim as unemployed. He has now signed on, losing £20 a week in the process. But his Disability Resettlement Officer says that he has little chance of finding work. The area has a very high rate of unemployment such that even well-qualified, white, non-disabled men have difficulties finding work. With his impairment, the chances are stacked against him. The agent is sympathetic. The young man has tried to make some money on the side by taping CDs and selling the tapes to friends. The agent has bought some of these tapes for a couple of pounds a time. She talks to the man and his mother for a while.

4.57   No answer at this call.

5.00   No answer at this call either. This is somewhat surprising because the agent is not visiting this address to collect money but to pay it back! The man has overpaid by mistake and the agent owed him £12.75. He knows that the money is coming and yet he is still not there. The agent remarks how this shows that people are sometimes genuinely out and are not just trying to avoid her.

5.03   A relatively new customer. She is friendly but only deals with the agent on the doorstep. The agent is equally friendly without seeming to be false or pushy.

5.08   A man comes out of his house to greet the agent. He hands over his book and money there and then. They talk for a while. His daughter, who no longer lives at home, is also a customer of the same agent. The agent is relieved that she is not asked in to the house. She likes this customer and would not want to appear rude by refusing to enter but the house smells rather unpleasant and she finds it uncomfortable.

5.15   This customer is a long-standing friend of the agent. They actually went to the same school. They chat about the customer's mother who had her 70th birthday recently. The agent had got her a card because she had known her for some time and sees her in church occasionally. The agent talks to the customer's young son.

5.25   A new customer – but no-one answers the door. This man has moved into the area and so been transferred from a different branch. The agent has not met him yet and does not know what time will be convenient. She will keep trying to call at different times to see if she can catch him in.

5.30   Another knock which is not answered. But the agent says that this customer is a good payer and she is confident that the customer will be in and pay next week.

5.40   A couple with children. They have just got back from a four week holiday. They had made no provision to make any of the £31.50 payments during those weeks. Before they went on holiday they borrowed a few hundred pounds and so far the agent had not had any repayments. How would they react now? The woman answers the door and asks the agent in. She has just returned from her uncle's funeral and has been drinking.

The agent tells her that her line manager has asked her to get more than one week's payment from the customer, to make up for the missed payments. The customer feels rather put out by this and says that she had no intention of paying any more than £31.50 that week. She complains that the loans are expensive enough anyway so she is not prepared to pay more. The agent asks, fairly meekly, if the customer would consider paying just £1 more a week on top of the £31.50. But the customer refuses. The agent says that her line manager would not be too happy about it. The customer replies,

Tell him to sod off ... I'm paying enough already. I'm not paying any more!

She tells the agent to send the line manager round if he is unhappy.

The agent is relatively self-controlled during this call, but she is angry when she gets back to the car. She feels that she has given them a loan in good faith and that they are not sticking to their side of the bargain. They had known the terms of the loan and if they thought it was too expensive they should have gone elsewhere. They had paid well before getting the loan but as soon as they got it they started missing several payments. The agent had expected them to make some gesture towards making up for the misses. She did not want to show her anger because the couple had been good customers in the past and she did not want to ruin her relationship with them. The line manager would probably make a visit.

5.44 The next call that the agent usually made at this stage was to a young woman who had recently been made homeless and was now in a bed & breakfast hotel. But she had not left the address.

5.45 The final call. Regular payers who never 'let her down'.

The agent had made a total of 39 calls in 5 hours and 45 minutes. This averages out to one call every 8 minutes. This included two calls of 40 minutes each. One of these was the stop for tea and the other was a stop to issue two new loans to a couple. Some calls were very short where the door was not answered by the customer or business was dealt with on the doorstep. But the average time includes all the travelling to and from each call.

Appendix 2

Methods of Research

Since the focus of the research was on the nature of the relationship between lender and borrower, we considered it essential for the research to be qualitative in nature. As well as interviewing lenders and borrowers separately, we decided that some form of observation work would be useful so that the relationship between borrower and lender could, to some extent, be seen directly by the researcher. Since this research involved some observation work, several classic studies and textbooks were consulted for guidance (Whyte 1955, Smith and Grey 1983, Becker 1970, Schatzman and Strauss 1973, Burgess 1984, Hammersley and Atkinson 1993). The advisory group also gave advice about the methods of research being undertaken.

Sampling the companies, collectors and customers
One of the first questions in the research design concerned the number of companies, collectors and customers to be included in the research. It is always difficult with qualitative research to know how many cases will be sufficient to provide both the depth and breadth of information which is required. We decided to include 8 collectors in the study so that we could cover different types of company and collector.

Since the six largest companies employ so many more collectors than the small or medium-sized ones, we decided to include six companies in the research – two large, two medium and two small – and take two collectors from each of the two large companies.

The next issue to resolve was identifying these companies and gaining their cooperation. From previous knowledge of the industry, we knew that the best way was to enlist the support of their trade association, CCA UK. After some discussion, CCA agreed to cooperate.

In order for us to select the sample, CCA sent us a list of their members. The list gave details of the size of the company including the number of employees, the nature of the company's business – whether cash loans, goods or vouchers, and the geographical location of the company.

The researchers chose two of the large companies from the list of five CCA giants and these agreed to take part in the research. CCA made the first contact with these companies, asking them if they would take part in the research. Both agreed.

The researchers then selected about ten medium-sized companies. These were given to CCA who were instructed to start with companies at the top of the list and work down it until they were able to gain agreement from two companies. A similar process occurred with the small companies. The reason for oversampling the small and medium-sized companies was that the fieldwork had to be conducted at a very particular time to fit in with the researcher's other committments and so CCA had to arrange the details very quickly.

Having selected the six companies, it was then possible to select the eight collectors. In the small companies, the managers were also the collectors of the company and so there was no second selection process. In the medium-sized and large companies, the researcher specified which area they wished to work in. For example, we might have specified that we wanted to include a collector who worked in Clapham. This meant that the company had very little opportunity to direct us to particular collectors as there would be few collectors who worked in these areas. The areas were selected to reflect a range of socio-geographic factors – for example, inner city, suburb, small town. Practical factors were also important since the fieldwork involved long periods in the North, Midlands and South.

Having selected the eight collectors, the 31 customers were selected after the observation work. This enabled the researcher to select a reasonably representative number in terms of demographic factors and the different customer types. For example, people were selected to reflect the fact that some customers always paid the full repayment every week, some missed and some paid reduced amounts every week.

On meeting customers during the observation work, a letter was handed to them, explaining the nature of the research and the possibility that they would be called on again and asked for an interview. This letter was on PSI headed paper and stressed the independent nature of the research. A copy is included in the back of this report.

In the field

Having selected and gained the cooperation of the companies, senior managers were contacted by the researchers. These managers were visited and information was collected from them about their companies. The researcher also took this opportunity to explain the aims and methods of research in more detail. In the medium and large companies this was usually the point at which the collectors were selected for inclusion in the study.

Each company was researched in turn so that once the managers from the first company had been met and interviewed, the collector/s from that company were observed and interviewed, and then the customers from that company were interviewed. The second company was then approached and so on.

One of the potential problems with participant observation is the researcher effect. Even if a researcher is only observing the activities of others, those being observed may deviate from their usual activities because of the presence of the researcher. In order to reduce or at least understand the researcher effect, it is important to be aware of the impression which is given by the researcher.

Some of the collectors had been told that I was 'from the government' and was accompanying them to check up on the company practice. Partly because of this, some of the collectors seemed slightly nervous about my presence and seemed to feel that they were being judged – which, in a way, they were. I explained about the organisation I worked for and the nature and purpose of the research. I also reassured them that I would not be feeding back any information about them to their managers. I also stressed that I was just there to look and learn about what they did, not to praise or criticise.

From the reaction of the customers, there was no indication that the collectors acted any differently in my presence. And during interviews with customers when the collector was not present, they all said that the visit I saw was a typical one.

I also asked the collectors if they thought my presence had affected the customers. A typical response was,

> *No I don't think so because you didn't come across that you were watching them or interested in them. I think if you had gone in sort of*

in a suit, it would have immediately put barriers up. But when I just said, 'this is Karen' – I didn't say, 'this is Mrs such-and-such' ... If I'd made you seem very important ... If they thought you were someone really important and they thought you were checking on them, they would definitely have put the barriers up.

All of the collectors introduced me as Karen and said that I was just finding out about the company and how it worked. This seemed to put customers at ease since they thought that I was interested in the company rather than them. At a convenient moment I handed them the letter which explained the research.

Some of the customers seemed initially concerned when they saw me because they thought I was taking over the round from their usual collector. Most seemed relieved to be told that this was not the case.

At a convenient point, either before or after the observation work, the collectors were interviewed. Customers were revisited after the end of the observation period. One customer refused outright to give an interview saying that she was very happy with the service provided by the company and did not have any more to say than that. Three people originally gave me a time when I could come back and interview them but were out when I called. Subsequent calls were unsuccessful in finding them at home. Apart from that, every customer that I found at home gave an interview.

Customers were given £10 as a thank you for taking part in the research. Collectors were also given £10 as a thank you for their time.

There was a concern that customers might indentify me very closely with their company and collector and so be wary of being critical. So at the beginning of the interview, I made a point of stressing confidentiality by confirming that I was not from the company and would not be seeing the collector again.

The fieldwork was carried out in two waves. The first wave took place in late July/early August 1993. This involved one of the large companies. Managers were interviewed, two collectors were observed and interviewed and eight interviews were conducted with customers.

Following this wave, and in consultation with the Joseph Rowntree Foundation advisory group, topic guides and other fieldwork materials were amended. Copies of the fieldwork documents are included at the end of this report.

The second wave of fieldwork then took part from August until November 1993.

Data collection

The interviews with managers, collectors and customers were tape-recorded except for two cases where customers preferred not to have their interviews taped. Detailed noted were taken at the time of the interview. There was also one occasion where the tape recorder broke. This was discovered immediately after leaving the interview and so detailed notes were taken at that point.

During the observation work, data was collected in a number of ways. For the pilot, there was a pro forma which enabled me to make notes for every call made by the collector. I wrote down the time of arrival at the call, the time of departure, and other details of the customer and call. For example, I noted the family type, whether someone missed a payment, where the call took place and so on. These notes were made in the collector's car between calls as it might have appeared intrusive to take notes while in someone's house. It was not easy to keep records for each call since the time in the car usually amounted to a minute or two during which time I would be fumbling with my seat belt, trying to get my pen and find the right sheet of paper. After consulting my advisory group, I started using a tape recorder in the car and dictated similar information. This also enabled me to tape conversations with the collector about customers after we had visited them. I also had a checklist with me of items to keep in mind during the observation work.

At the end of each day of observation work, I made notes based on my memory of anything which was not tape-recorded. These notes were mainly descriptive but there were some reflections on what the data might be starting to say. There were also notes on methodological points.

I also kept a fieldwork diary of the times spent together with some details of how the fieldwork fitted into other parts of my life.

Data analysis

The large amount of data collected from different participants meant that analysis would have to be conducted in a very methodical way to avoid personal impressions and bias. Full transcripts were obtained on all tape-recorded interviews. These were then read and information transferred onto grids. Separate grids were constructed for managers, interviews with collectors, interviews with customers and observation work. Cards were also used to make the managament and assessment of the information even easier to handle.

As well as the problem of researcher bias, participant observation is prone to researchers 'going native' and seeing the issue at stake only from a particular point of view. To some extent, it is important to understand this point of view but it is also important to be able to see the issue from other perspectives. By talking independently to both collectors and customers this problem was largely overcome. But it has also been important in the analysis to double check to see if I have been overly sympathetic towards one particular group. There may also be a tendency to react against this by moving too far in the other direction and being unjustifiably negative. Being aware of the potential problem enables researchers to guard against any bias in analysis. As a further safeguard, PSI colleagues have, as far as they can, checked my analysis and interpretation.

Report writing

The major problem with the reporting of this observation work has been the importance of preserving confidentiality. Only eight collectors took part in the research. Managers in each of the companies know which of their collectors were involved. So there have been times in the reporting where I would might have wanted to say that a particular quote came from a female agent or an agent working in the North but this would have identified the person and so I have had to merely say, *A collector said ...* and *another collector commented ...*

There is less chance for customers to be identified since they were selected after the observation work and the collectors did not know which ones were interviewed. But the collectors know their customers very well and some personal information might identify them. So, again, I have tried not to link information about customers to the quotes. For example, we do not know the family background of the customer who said that her collector could *'charm the pants off the queen'*.

In September 1994, a workshop was held, funded by the Joseph Rowntree Foundation, during which members of the advisory group together with representatives from the industry, regulators and consumer groups discussed a draft report. This report has taken on board many of the comments made at that workshop.

Appendix 3

Fieldwork Documents

(i)   Topic guides

(ii) Checklist for observation work

(iii) Letter to customers

GUIDE A – INTERVIEWS WITH MANAGERS

1. Current position of the company
   - Is there an annual report or equivalent?
   - Financial information – turnover and profits

2. The company's product – check trading, moneylending etc
   - Why this product/product mix?
   - Any plans to diversify or consolidate?

3. The company's market and marketing
   - How many customers?
   - Profile of customers – age, sex, class, region, urban/rural turnover of customers
   - What is the turnover of customers?
   - How are new customers found?

4. The company's competitors
   - Where does the company stand in the overall market?

5. Structure and procedures of the company
   - Where are decisions made about lending?
   - How does credit assessment take place?
   - Conditions of the loan
     - Average/range of amounts, repayment periods
   - How are loans rescheduled?
   - (Regional differences)

6. The agents/travellers
   - How many agents?
   - Profile of agents – age, sex, class
   - Employment type – hours, days, length of service
   - Recruitment/training and supervision/assessment
   - Turnover
   - What makes a good/bad agent
   - How many customers per agent?
   - Violence against agents?
   - Agents going native?

7. Brief history of the company
   - How have all these things changed since company started?
   - How have things changed in last 10 years – boom and bust

8. The future of the company

GUIDE B – INTERVIEWS WITH COLLECTORS BEFORE/ AFTER VISITS

1. The practicalities of the job
   - What hours and days do they work? Why?
     - Do these vary? Days, weeks, seasons
   - How much do they collect/lend out each week?
   - How much do they earn from the job?
     - Salary/commission/hourly rate?

2. A brief life and work history
   - Age, family background, where they live
     - Current family situation
   - Education, training and work history

3. Entry into moneylending
   - What attracted them to the work?
   - When did they start moneylending/check trading?
     - Why and how?
   - What training did they receive?

4. A career in moneylending
   - Has their job changed since they started? How?
   - What makes a good agent?
   - What do they like/dislike about their job?
     - What makes it worthwhile?
     - Ever wanted to give it up?
     - What have been the best/worst times or experiences?
   - Any experience of violence?

5. The company/managers they work for
   - How many companies/managers have they worked for?
     - Which have been the best/worst to work for?
   - What contact/relationship do they have with the company/ managers they work for? Eg Supervision, assessement?
   - How much do they earn? Incentives? Effect?
   - Do they know/meet other agents?
   - What do they know about other local companies? Or other types of credit in the area?

6. The customers
   - Customer profile
     - How many calls/customers do they have?
     - Profile of customers – age, sex, class
     - How would they divide their customers up?
   - Turnover and recruitment of customers
     - Family/social networks
   - How much business do they have?
   - What do they take into account when deciding whether to lend money?
     - How much autonomy do they have in making these decisions?
     - When would/have they refused loans? What happened?
     - Have they ever lent money and then regretted it? What happened?
   - What do they feel/do if someone has difficulty repaying?
     - Are there 'genuine' reasons for not paying?
   - What is a good/bad customer?
     - How can they tell if a new customer is going to be good/bad?
   - What is the ideal relationship to have with a customer?
     - What is the balance between business and personal relationship?
   - Which are their favourite/least favourite customers?
     - Why?

AFTER OBSERVATION WORK ASK:
   - Was the round any different from usual – either in how the collector or customers acted or just unusual circumstances?

GUIDE C – INTERVIEWS WITH CUSTOMERS

1. First use of this company
    *   How did they first hear about the company?
        –   When did they first use it?
        –   How did they get in touch initially?
    *   What were their family/financial circumstances?
    *   What were the details of the loan?
        –   Type of credit
        –   Reason for use
        –   Amount
    *   Why did they use this form of credit?
        –   What was money used for?
        –   Alternatives to borrowing from this company? – save, defer, other credit options
        –   What would they have done if this type of credit had not been available?

2. Overall pattern of use
    *   Have they used any other similar companies?
        –   Repeat 1 and compare companies
        –   Do they know about any other companies?
    *   How often have they used this type of credit since the first time? Do they top up their credit regularly or do they use it periodically?
    *   What type of credit have they used?
        –   Compare goods to vouchers to cash
    *   Have they ever been refused a loan? In what circumstances?

3. Current use of weekly collected credit
    *   See card/book records
        –   How many loans?
        –   When was taken out?
        –   How much for?
        –   What used for?
        –   Which companies?
    *   What would they do if this credit was not available?
        –   Save, defer, borrow from another source – where?

- Do they ever have difficulties finding the money for repayments? What happens? If short of money, how do they feel? What do they do? What are priorities for payment?
- What will happen when this loan ends? What does the agent say?
  - If want another loan, what happens?
- If they were not paying £x a week to the collector, what would they do with the money?
- How would they feel/what would they do if doorstep collection was replaced by a different payment system?

4. Relationship with current agent
    - How long have they been with this agent?
      - What do they know about the agent? Eg licensed? Name? Telephone?
    - Is the visit I saw typical?
      - When does the agent call?
      - How long do they stay?
      - What do they talk about?
    - What is the agent like? How does he/she compare to other agents?

5. Other credit use
    - Are they currently making repayments or have they previously made repayments on other credit commitments, like:
      - Mail order catalogue – have they ever been an agent?
      - Arrangement/HP with a shop/fuel board
      - Credit unions
      - Loan from employer, Social Fund
      - Loan from bank, building society
      - Bank account/overdraft
      - Loan from finance company (eg HP)
      - Credit cards
      - Borrow from family/friends?

FOR EACH COMMITMENT, ASK:
- What was the money spent on?
- Who they borrowed from/when/how much?
- How much and how frequent are the payments?
- Any difficulties with payments? Why? What happened?

FOR ALL THOSE NOT USED, ASK:
- Have they ever considered using other types of credit?
- Why have they not used other types of credit?
- Are they available to the respondent?

6. Attitudes to credit
   - What are the pros and cons of this type of credit?
   - How do they feel about using this form of credit?
     - Especially compared with other forms?
   - When would they use one rather than the other?

7. Family use and opinions
   - Do members of the family, friends and neighbours use this type of credit?
   - What do these people think about the respondent using this type of credit?
   - Have they ever introduced anyone or been introduced to this type of credit by anyone else?
     - Would they recommend it to someone? Why/why not?

8. Income and outgoings
   - Establish age, economic activity and income of each member of family and any changes in last three years
   - Establish household outgoings
     - Who is responsible for budgeting?
     - What do they do when bills arrive?
     - What are priorities?
       - Any difficulties paying?
       - Any arrears at the moment? What are they?
     - Do they save any money?
   - What are their attitudes to money and budgeting?
     - Do they have a bank/b soc account?
     - What do they think about saving?
     - Do they worry about bills/money/debt?
   - How well do they feel they are managing at the moment?

CHECKLIST FOR OBSERVATION WORK

The local context
    Locality
    Timing – season/day/hour
    Weather

The practicalities of doing the round
    The structure of the round
    Practical problems eg parking/traffic
    'Incidents' – expected and unexpected

How collectors and customers present themselves
    Physical appearance eg clothing
    Accent, speech
    Attitudes towards eachother
    Personality/behaviour

The interaction
    Business vs social aspects of the interaction
    Topics of conversation – levels of intimacy/formality
    Where the agent stands/sits
    Who deals with the collector

POLICY STUDIES INSTITUTE

Park Village East
don, NWI 3SR
0171-387 2171
:: 0171-388 0914

September 1993

Dear sir/madam,

I have been accompanying your collector as part of a survey about weekly collected credit companies. More and more people are using these companies and yet little is known about the type of service they give.

The survey is being conducted by myself and Elaine Kempson at the Policy Studies Institute (PSI). PSI is an independent organisation specialising in research on issues such as housing, employment, social security and credit.

We would like to talk to some customers to find out what they think about the company they use. If you are happy to give an interview, any information you give me will be treated in the strictest confidence. No-one from the company or anywhere else will know what you tell me. In order to thank you for your time, there is a £10 gift for everyone who gives an interview.

I hope that you will be able to help me with this survey.

Yours sincerely,

Karen Rowlingson

red Charity No. 313819
mited by guarantee
ation No. 779698
g. No. GB 239 1031 87